Bleeding Hands, Weeping Stone

TRUE STORIES OF DIVINE WONDERS, MIRACLES, AND MESSAGES

Bleeding Hands, Weeping Stone

TRUE STORIES OF DIVINE WONDERS, MIRACLES, AND MESSAGES

Elizabeth Ficocelli

Saint Benedict Press
Charlotte, North Carolina
2009

ISBN: 978-1-935302-31-5

Cover design by Tony Pro

Printed and Bound in the United States of America

SAINT
BENEDICT
PRESS

SAINT BENEDICT PRESS, LLC
Charlotte, North Carolina
2010

Publisher's Note

Some of the miraculous phenomena related in this book are hundreds of years old; some of them are modern-day, and involve persons still living or events still alleged to be occurring. We believe that God didn't stop working miracles long ago, in some more-credulous age, but that he continues working them in the world today, even (or especially) in our age of widespread unbelief. For this reason we think it's important at least to report on some of the more-reputable miraculous claims of our time.

The Church may condemn alleged miracles, or declare them to be non-supernatural, at any time, but it will never give its approval until after —sometimes long after—they have ceased, so that they might be evaluated in their entirety. Some recent phenomena included in this book, therefore, may not have yet received Church approval; some, perhaps, never will. Saint Benedict Press makes no claims as to their authenticity. But at the time of publication, none of them have been condemned, and each bears at least the primary mark that all authentic miracles must bear: they humbly point the way to Christ and his Church.

For Father Samuel Leonard,
  God's special miracle to our family

E.F.

Contents

PREFACE

Several years ago, I had the pleasure of taking two of my teenage sons to hear Catholic speaker Jason Evert at a local parish. Jason's an accomplished author and speaker best known for his lively and engaging presentations on chastity for teen audiences. This particular evening, however, his talk was titled, "What's So Great about Being Catholic?"

For the next hour or so, in his animated and humorous style, Jason named plenty of terrific reasons for being Catholic. He talked about the sacraments, the Pope, the universality of the Church; but it was when he began to touch upon the *mystical* side of the Faith that I noticed the greatest reaction from his teenage audience. As he tantalized them with stories of consecrated hosts that have actually bled during Mass, dead bodies that have never rotted, and saints that could fly, the audience was drawn in immediately. The more he talked, the more they listened. I watched as they leaned further and further on the edges of their seats. Their mouths dropped open in astonishment, and they turned to look at their neighbors with shaking heads and widened eyes.

I knew exactly how these young people were feeling that night. These were precisely the kinds of stories that sparked my own interest when I entered the Catholic Church as a young adult in the early '80s. I remember reading about miracles like these and being completely blown away, because such things were *never* talked about in my Protestant upbringing. Discovering how God reveals himself to his people in such extraordinary and wonderful ways was like stumbling upon a hidden treasure that would forever leave an impression on me. It made my new Catholic faith even more mysterious, intriguing, attractive, and respectable.

A quick poke of my neighbor's elbow interrupted my thoughts. It was a good friend I had invited to hear Jason speak. "Elizabeth," she whispered insistently in my ear. "I've been a Catholic all my life. *Why have I never heard these things before?*" I didn't have an answer for my friend that night, but her question would rattle around my brain long after. That evening, a seed was planted. It had become clear to me that there was a real need and a ready audience—young and not so young, Catholic and even non-Catholic—to hear once again the stories of our mystical faith that in recent decades have stopped being told.

My thinking is this: if God has gone through all this trouble to get our attention in such creative and marvelous ways, the least we can do is sit up and take notice.

Introduction

Welcome to the Age of Miracles

Thanks to the explosion of computer technology in the past fifteen years or so, we are living in a pretty amazing time. If our great, great, great, *great* grandparents could have seen how computers would absolutely revolutionize human existence in the modern age, they probably would have called it miraculous.

For those who have grown up with it, computer technology seems perfectly normal and even hum-drum. We take for granted how it has affected almost every aspect of our lives: how we communicate, how we work, how we drive, how we shop, how we eat—and even how we are entertained. Thanks to the magic of computer-generated special effects, for example, most anything a screenwriter or director dreams up can be made to appear on a TV or movie screen. And the audiences eat it up faster than they eat their buckets of popcorn! Just look at the top grossing movies of all time—the real blockbusters. You won't find quiet films about two lovers in the countryside on the list. The big winners are movies packed with space ships and dragons and magic and monsters and super-human strength and mind powers. The more

fantastic the idea and the more outlandish the effects, the
more movie critics and audiences alike rave, "Awesome!"
"Mind-Boggling!" "Unreal!"

And you know what? That's exactly what it is.
Unreal.

Now, I can't blame people for being drawn to things
that are unreal. After all, reality can be pretty discourag-
ing, even downright scary at times. That's a fact. But what
if I were to tell you there are *lots* of amazing, unexplainable, out-of-this-world phenomena that have happened in
the past—and continue to happen today—all without the
help of computer technology and special effects? Things
that are beyond belief and yet one hundred percent *real*?
That's exactly the kind of stories you'll find in this book.

Now, these aren't the kinds of stories we usually hear at Sunday Mass, or in religion class. Many of
them are like hidden treasures, stored away in the attic
of the Faith. But that doesn't mean they're not important. Fact is, our Catholic Faith is full of fantastic and
mystical (and true) tales. If you don't believe me, crack
open the Bible and start reading. I guarantee it won't be
long before you stumble upon something supernatural,
like Abraham and the burning bush that talks. Or the
prophet Elijah being served his dinner in the desert by
ravens. Or a small shepherd boy named David taking out
a giant with a stone and a leather strap. Then there's the
matter of seas parting, bread falling from heaven, city
walls crumbling at the sound of horns and voices...and
we haven't even gotten to the New Testament yet. That's
when things *really* get interesting! Like a young girl
named Mary getting pregnant by the Holy Spirit in order
to bear the Son of God. Or a star leading wise men from
the east to a little town called Bethlehem, many countries
away. Or the awesome signs and wonders Jesus and his

apostles performed, such as healing the sick, multiplying food, and even raising the dead.

Certainly, God's becoming one of us and walking around the earth to show us how much he loves has to be the most amazing miracle of all. But it wasn't the last. God is still here with us. Maybe he's not as visible as Jesus was to people of Israel, but he's still very active and present in the world. Through his living word, the Bible, and the sacraments of the Church, he continues to teach and sanctify us. And every now and then, at times when our faith needs an extra push, he steps in and really catches our attention with something so awesome, so mind-boggling, that it seems... *unreal.*

How exactly does God do this? Here are a few of his attention-grabbing techniques:

- Real human flesh or blood appearing right on the altar in the middle of Mass
- Raw, open sores that look just like the wounds of Jesus, mysteriously popping up on a person's hands, feet, head, and side
- The body of a holy person refusing to rot—even hundreds of years after death
- Saints demonstrating astonishing abilities to heal, read hearts, predict the future, glow, or even levitate like a magician
- Visions of Jesus, Mary, the angels, or saints giving the world messages of encouragement and warning
- Statues and other artwork actually weeping tears of oil, water, and blood

Sound more like a ghost story than religion? I can assure you, it's not. These are true and incredible gifts that God has been giving us for centuries. The Church painstakingly evaluates such occurrences before carefully giving its stamp of approval, as a way to protect and nurture the faithful. Authenticated miracles like the ones listed above have helped many people regain their faith at times when the world was working hard to lure them away with lies and empty promises. And, because the world is still doing this, perhaps more than ever, such remarkable events are still happening today, often to the surprise and confusion of modern scientists. So dare now to venture up to the attic with me and uncover the treasures that lie waiting for you, filled with all their wonder and weirdness. I think you'll agree. We're living in a pretty amazing time.

CHAPTER 1

Jesus, in the Flesh:
Eucharistic Miracles

So Jesus said to them, "Very truly I tell you, unless
you eat the flesh of the Son of Man and drink his
blood, you have no life in you. Those who eat my flesh
and drink my blood have eternal life, and I will raise
them up on the last day; for my flesh is true food and
my blood is true drink."

—John 6:54–56

As you can tell from the above quote (and if you
skipped over it, no cheating—go back and read it),
the Eucharist is nothing to mess around with. It's real
flesh, it's real blood—and it gives us eternal life. Even
though it looks, smells, and tastes like bread or wine, at
the moment of consecration a real and important change
has taken place, and we, too, are changed by partaking in
this holy meal. The Eucharist is so vital to our faith that
Jesus not only invited us to eat it, he *commanded* us to.

1

Wow. To think how many times we've been distracted at this part of Mass, failing to recognize the miracle going on right in front of our eyes! It's sad to say, but if you look at the faces of those who receive the Eucharist regularly today, many seem to be pretty unimpressed—even bored—with the whole thing. Well, that's nothing new. Throughout Christian history there have been people who questioned whether the Eucharist was truly the body and blood of Jesus, or even whether Jesus was present in the Eucharist at all. Others got in the habit of receiving the sacrament when they weren't deserving of it—even when they were in a state of serious sin. Still others stopped receiving it altogether.

On certain such occasions, when the eyes of faith have grown dim to the mystery and miracle of the Eucharist, God has taken it upon himself to intervene miraculously, giving us a glimpse into the truth about the Eucharist in a way we can appreciate with our human eyes. Once in a while, just a very few special times, he has turned consecrated bread into physical human flesh and consecrated wine into physical human blood. He has also been known at times to give the Eucharist special power to survive fires, floods, thievery, and decay.

These rare and spectacular events are known as *Eucharistic miracles.* Hundreds of such miracles have been reported throughout history and many of them have been documented and approved by the Catholic Church. You can find proof of these baffling mysteries preserved in churches around the world, a lasting testimony to the fact that yes, it's really Jesus in the Eucharist.

The Disbelieving Priest

Probably the earliest case of a Eucharist miracle, and one of the most famous on record, came about because of the doubts of a man from the town of Lanciano, Italy, sometime during the 700s. It may surprise or even shock you to know that our Doubting Thomas was a Catholic priest, who despite being a priest was really wrestling with the concept of Jesus' being truly present in the Eucharist. No matter how hard he prayed, the priest could not rise above his doubts. That's when God stepped in.

One day, as the priest lifted the Host at the moment of consecration, the round, white wafer was instantly surrounded by a ring of visible flesh. At the same moment, the consecrated wine in the chalice on the altar formed into five jelly-like pellets of human blood. Talk about a transformation! The astonished priest and congregation at once begged God to forgive them for their weak faith. They repented on the spot, and the faith of the whole town was renewed. And just so they would never forget God's great gift, the miraculous flesh and blood were carefully enshrined in a beautiful *monstrance*, a fancy vessel made of precious materials, for future generations to adore.

Some twelve hundred years later, in 1971 to be exact, modern scientists were given permission to study the still-preserved sacred specimens of Lanciano. The scientists confirmed that the container holding the Eucharistic Miracle was not airtight. Nor had any preservatives been added. Therefore, by logic, they should have deteriorated over the centuries. But somehow the specimens are still present and intact. The center of the host had dissolved, but the flesh along the outer edges remained.

The scientists examined it closer and determined that the flesh is from the wall of a human heart. Next, they looked at the five pellets of blood, which although dry and hard on the outside, were actually fluid on the inside. Samples taken from the pellets showed that the blood is human blood, type AB—the exact same kind found in the

The Eucharistic Miracle of Lanciano. Photo courtesy of the Sanctuary of the Eucharistico Miracle.

specimen of flesh. Even more astounding, the blood was shown to contain the same minerals, chemicals, and proteins as fresh human blood, *even though it was 1,250 years old*. How could that be? With God, all things are possible!

Repentance in Regensburg

In the year 1194, in a town called Regensburg, Germany, an unusual event took place. A woman who had received Communion decided to secretly remove the Host from her mouth (back then it was not permitted to receive in the hand) and take it home with her. She didn't mean any harm; she simply wanted to worship Jesus in her home. However, this practice was strictly forbidden.

Once the woman arrived home, she carefully enclosed the Host between two pieces of wax to protect it.

After a few years passed, the woman began to feel guilty about what she had done, and she confessed the matter to her priest. He promptly accompanied her to her home and returned the Host to its rightful place in the church. However, when he opened the wax container to retrieve the Host, the priest was shocked to discover that it had partially turned to flesh! He immediately summoned the bishop, who ordered that the Host and the wax container be placed in the cathedral.

But the miracle wasn't over yet. Once in the cathedral, the Host began to expand in size until it actually cracked the wax casing. A larger and more appropriate container was constructed in gold, and a feast has been celebrated every year since in honor of the miracle. It is said that many healings have been reported to take place during these celebrations.

The Cheating Husband

In the town of Santarem, Portugal, in the 1200s, another woman decided to remove a consecrated Host from church. But her reasons were a bit more selfish. She was discouraged by her husband's unfaithfulness and had consulted a local sorceress or fortuneteller. The sorceress promised she could help the woman with her problem, but it would come at a price: one consecrated Host. But as soon as the woman left the church with the Host hidden discreetly in her veil, it began to bleed heavily. People on the street tried to stop the woman to help her, thinking she had injured herself, but she ran away from them to her home and hid the bloody mess in a trunk in her bedroom.

That night, a strange light glowed from inside the trunk, waking the couple up. Frightened by her crime, the woman confessed to her husband. Together, they knelt before the trunk in awe and adoration until dawn, when they summoned the parish priest. News of the miracle spread far and wide. The woman's house was converted to a little chapel, and each year, the miraculous Host is processed from the chapel to the church in memory of the wonder God had done in the town. I'm not sure about the husband, but I have a feeling he stopped cheating after that.

The Fisherman and the Fire

A century later, in Amsterdam, there lived a fisherman who was quite ill. His wife feared for his life and called for the local priest to give her husband Last Rites and Holy Communion. Once the priest had left, the dying fisherman started to cough so violently that the Host flew out of his mouth and landed on the floor. The wife, in a moment of unclear thinking, grabbed the Host and threw it into the fire. She instantly regretted her hasty action, but it was too late. The flames had swallowed it.

The next morning, as she was sifting though the ashes, the woman was shocked to discover the Host in perfect condition. In wonder, she carefully wrapped the precious item in linen and placed it in a chest. Then she called for the priest, who decided to return the Host to the church quietly to avoid any scandal. Imagine the woman's surprise when she found the Host back in her linen drawer the following day! She ran at once to tell the priest, who had already discovered that the Host was missing from the church. He realized then that God did not wish to keep this miracle a secret. Therefore, a large public procession was organized, and the Host was taken from the couple's home to the church in proper fashion. The fisherman recovered his health, and in gratitude for his healing and for the miracle, he turned his home into a chapel, where the miraculous Host was eventually enshrined. This is not the end of the story, however. One hundred years later, the chapel burned to the ground when the entire city of Amsterdam was engulfed by fire. People tried their best to rescue the Host, but it was impossible. How joyful they were the following day when they found the Host and monstrance perfectly safe among the ashes! These two Eucharistic miracles and the pilgrimages they attracted helped transform Amsterdam from an obscure fishing village into the major port city it is today.

The Holy Knight

In Seefeld, Austria, in 1384 lived a knight named Oswald Milser, famed throughout the land as a man full of power... and full of himself. He unintentionally left his mark on the history of Eucharistic miracles one Holy Thursday, when he and his band of armed men forced their way into a local parish. The arrogant knight demanded that he be given the large Host, the one normally reserved for the priest. At the sight of Oswald's sword drawn and ready, the priest became frightened and reluctantly placed the Host on the knight's waiting tongue. At that very moment, the concrete floor Oswald was standing on suddenly and mysteriously softened, and the surprised knight sank into it up to his knees. Struggling to get free, he gripped the altar with two hands, but it too gave way to his grasp and his hands plunged deeply into the stone. Oswald begged the priest to remove the Host, which by now had turned bright red, and once he did, the floor and altar became hard again. The bewildered knight pulled himself out of the holes and made a beeline to the nearest monastery where he made a complete and heartfelt confession. They say he was converted and lived a holy life from that point on. Today the church is named after St. Oswald, and the holes in the floor and in the altar, still visible, continue to make a deep impression on all who visit.

A *Flood in France*

In the autumn of 1433, the river Sorgue in Avignon, France, flooded to dangerous levels. Along the banks of the angry river sat a little church in which the Blessed Sacrament was exposed twenty-four hours a day. Fearing that the Eucharist might get swept away in the floodwaters, two Franciscan friars jumped in a boat and rowed their way precariously to the little church. When they arrived on the scene, they found that the water had already entered the chapel to a depth of four feet. To their amazement and joy, however, the waters inside had mysteriously parted, like the Red Sea, from the door of the church right up to the altar where the Blessed Sacrament was displayed. Everything in the passageway was completely dry. It was a miracle!

Every year on November 30, the Franciscans reenact the day that God demonstrated his power and might over water. And from what I hear, people come flooding in to hear the story. (Okay, that was a bad one!)

Stop, Thief!

Three centuries later, in Siena, Italy, everybody in town was celebrating the vigil of the Feast of the Assumption, the occasion when Mary was taken body and soul into heaven. Everybody, that is, except for a few sneaky thieves. They crept into the empty Church of St. Francis and picked the lock on the tabernacle. They stole the *ciborium*, the covered golden vessel that held the consecrated Hosts. Perhaps they felt guilty about their crime, because the next morning one of the townspeople found the golden ciborium in the street. The Hosts, however, were nowhere to be found. The whole town prayed in anguish, worried about the precious Body of Jesus being in the hands of the thieves.

Two days later, the parish priest noticed something white sticking out of the poor box at the back of church. He realized it was a Host. When the box was opened, he found the rest of the missing Hosts, although they had become quite soiled by the dust and cobwebs in the box. The priest carefully cleaned the Hosts as best he could and decided not to consume them, but to let them naturally deteriorate. This must not have been God's plan, however, because the Hosts remained fresh, shiny, and pleasantly scented, despite the passage of time, and today, more than 250 years later, the Hosts remain miraculously preserved. I doubt you could say the same for the thieves.

This Ought to Make You Smile

France was the scene of another Eucharistic miracle in the year 1822, this time in the town of Bordeaux. In a small church called the Chapel of the Ladies of Loreto, a priest, the altar servers, some religious sisters, as well as the congregation were all privileged one day, as the Blessed Sacrament was set out on the altar to be adored, to see a vision of Jesus. It was not a static image, like a photograph, but a living, moving likeness of Jesus, including his head, chest, and arms. He gazed out upon his people from the center of the large monstrance on the altar. He wore a dark red cloak over his shoulders, and his right hand was raised in blessing. Witnesses testified that the smiling image of their Savior lasted for about twenty minutes. I'm sure the witnesses were smiling back!

Volcanic Interruption

The start of the twentieth century was celebrated with two Eucharistic miracles that involved natural disasters. In 1902, not far from a village called Morne-Rouge in the Caribbean island of Martinique, a massive volcano erupted. As the villagers watched Mount Pelée spew ash and lava in all directions, they rushed to their parish to pray for God's help to spare them from catastrophe. The priest responded quickly. As people hurried to the confessionals, he gave them a general absolution or pardon for their sins. Next, he placed a consecrated Host in a monstrance on the altar and instructed the people to pray. As the villagers of Morne-Rouge adored the Lord, they saw a vision of the Sacred Heart of Jesus, to whom they had a special devotion. They took this as a sign that their prayers had been heard—and they were, for Morne-Rouge was not destroyed that day. Many other villages in the area were not so fortunate.

Quake and Quiver

Four years later, in 1906, another disaster struck, this time in Tumaco, Columbia. A large undersea earthquake lasting ten minutes caused the water to swell into an enormous tsunami, a series of gigantic and destructive waves. (You may recall the tsunami of 2007, which sent deadly waves throughout Indonesia, leveling villages, towns, and cities, and killing hundreds of thousands of people.) The frightened people of Tumaco hurried straight to their local priest and begged him to lead them in a procession with the Blessed Sacrament as their protection. The group arrived at the edge of the sea and prayed devoutly. The priest lifted the monstrance in the air and made the Sign of the Cross with it. As the enormous wall of water rushed toward them, it seemed to halt and then recede, miraculously sparing the village and its inhabitants.

Drip, Drip

A little closer to our time, a notable event occurred in the town of Stich, in what was then West Germany. It was the year 1970 and a visiting priest from Switzerland was celebrating Mass when he noticed one, then two red spots on the white cloth underneath the chalice. He thought perhaps the chalice had a leak. After Mass, when he was not able to find a source of moisture from either the cup or the altar, he decided to have the stains investigated. Scientific tests proved that the spots were blood from a human male. One month later, a second miracle occurred when the same priest visited the parish again to celebrate Mass. At the time of consecration, four spots of blood appeared on the cloth beneath the chalice. This time each one contained a small cross in the center. A different lab was asked to examine these spots and once again they were confirmed to be human blood. Two miracles— what a spot of luck!

Face It, It's a Miracle

Eucharist miracles continue to happen, even in this millennium. As recently as April 28, 2001, a Eucharistic miracle began to reveal itself at the Malankara Catholic

Eucharistic Miracle of Chirattakonam. Photo courtesy of Mankara Catholic Church.

Church in a town in India known as Chirattakonam. The parish priest and his congregation were doing their usual novena prayer to St. Jude, the patron saint for hopeless causes. The Eucharist was displayed in a monstrance for adoration. During that time, the priest noticed three spots appear on the Blessed Sacrament. He asked the members of his congregation if they could see it too, and they said they could. Afterward, not sure what to make of it, the priest locked the Host in the tabernacle for safekeeping.

A week later, as he was preparing to celebrate the Mass, the priest opened the tabernacle and removed the Host. By this time, an image of a human face had begun to emerge on the Eucharist. Again, the priest showed it to his people, and again they confirmed that they, too, could see it. Together they prayed with the Eucharist before them, and as the congregation gazed upon it, the image grew clearer. Soon it transformed into the unmistakable face of a bearded man with long hair. The local bishop was consulted for his opinion, and he accepted it as miraculous, encouraging the congregation to pray and discern what God might be saying to them through this remarkable event.

Curiosities in Korea

Another report of a miracle happening in our time is the case of Julia Kim, a young housewife and mother of four children from Naju, Korea. In 1985, Julia was diagnosed with a serious form of cancer with no hope of survival. Her husband took her to a Catholic priest, who prayed with her, and soon she found herself completely healed. This incident inspired Julia to become Catholic.

At least twelve times between the years 1988 and 1996, a most unusual phenomenon happened to Julia as she received Holy Communion. Shortly after the Host was placed on her tongue, witnesses report that it swelled and turned into physical flesh and blood in the woman's mouth. I know that sounds impossible (not to mention unappealing), but many people have witnessed these miracles, including bishops and even the late Pope John Paul II during Julia's visit to Rome in 1995. As credible as these witnesses are, however, it is the local bishop whose approval matters most, according to Church rules. And Julia's bishop is simply not convinced. It seems that many priests and laypeople in Korea don't like all the attention that Julia seems to attract. They think the whole thing is old-fashioned and superstitious. It makes matters rather complicated.

In addition to Julia's curious Eucharistic Miracles, there are a number of other mysterious events surrounding this young woman. These include visions of Jesus and Mary with special messages for the world, a statue that weeps blood, numerous healings, and pronounced marks that appear on Julia's body known as the *stigmata*, or the wounds of Christ. (We'll be talking about peculiar events like these in upcoming chapters in this book.) While the debate continues about whether this modern day miracle is really a miracle at all, it has seemed to inspire a great deal of faith and passion among the people. Many are coming back to Church and the sacraments, and that is a kind of miracle in itself.

✠   ✠   ✠

So what do you think so far? Pretty wild, isn't it? And this is just a small sample of the incredible marvels that have been associated with the Eucharist through-out history. But here's the thing: as spectacular as these stories are, they still don't come close the miracle that happens at your parish and mine, every single day that Mass is celebrated (which is every day, by the way!). By that I mean the miracle of the king and creator of the universe who humbles and hides himself within the form of simple bread and wine so he can come to the people he loves and dwell with them in a special and intimate way. That, unquestionably, is the greatest miracle of all.

CHAPTER 2

Pierced by the Spirit: Stigmata

Henceforth let no man trouble me; for I bear on my body the marks of Jesus.

—Galatians 6:17

*I*magine having your hands and feet pierced by large iron nails. Your forehead punctured by three-inch pointy thorns sunk deep into your skull. Your back swollen by the sting of leather whips. And your side opened by the sharp point of a lance. This gruesome torture was the fate of Jesus Christ, our Lord and God, who willingly endured such unthinkable sufferings to save us from sin and death.

As we all know, Jesus won that bloody victory for us because three days later, he rose from the dead. Every Easter we sing happy songs about his Resurrection and then go home to eat chocolate bunnies and look for colored eggs. But the fact is, Jesus couldn't have made it to Easter

Sunday without going through Good Friday first. That's a hard truth for us, because it's not fun to dwell on all the gruesome details of Christ's suffering. Suffering, as a general rule, is something we try very hard to avoid. When we're hungry, we eat. When we're cold, we turn up the heat. And when we have a headache, we take an aspirin. Let's face it—we're all about comfort, not suffering.

There are some people, however, who have felt drawn to thinking quite deeply about Jesus' Passion. Perhaps they prayed about it for long periods of time in front of images of our tortured Savior and their hearts became inflamed with love and sympathy. In time, some of these special individuals found themselves so emotionally connected with Jesus that they even wanted to share in his suffering with their own bodies. In a way that's hard for us to understand, they were willing to endure real physical pain out of love for Jesus—not a pain they would inflict on themselves, or a pain that gave them some sort of sick pleasure, but a pain they would permit happen to them supernaturally, all for the love of Christ.

These people were so holy, they didn't want others to know how much they suffered. They didn't want their pain to be visible because they didn't want to draw attention to themselves. Yet sometimes, despite their wish to hide their suffering, God allowed real and painful lesions, just like the wounds that Christ suffered in his passion, to spontaneously erupt on a person's body and bleed for days, years, or even decades. This is perhaps one of the most bizarre and mystifying miracles of all, known as the stigmata.

It was St. Paul, in his letter to the Galatians, who first talked about bearing "the marks of Jesus." (That's the quote at the beginning of this chapter. Did you read it this time? If not, you know what to do...) Most Bible experts, however, don't believe that St. Paul was physically marked by the stigmata, since there are no other references to this in Scripture or in ancient documents. Most scholars believe he was talking in a figurative or symbolic sense. Quite probably, St. Paul was *relating* to Jesus' suffering, since he himself had been beaten many times and thrown into prison for preaching Christianity.

Francis Is First

The first person in history known to have truly borne Christ-like wounds on his body was St. Francis, in the year 1224. (You might remember him as the saint who befriended all the animals.) Francis was the son of a wealthy cloth merchant, and his mother came from nobility. As a youth, Francis loved the party life. This changed dramatically at the age of twenty, however, when he joined the local military to protect his hometown of Assisi, Italy, from an aggressive nearby city. Francis was captured by the enemy and thrown in prison for more than a year. During those months of hardship, isolation, and illness, something happened to that fun-loving and self-absorbed young man. When Francis was released, he had a change of heart about his priorities. Unable to continue his military career because of poor health, he spent more time in prayer and fasting and solitude. He discovered that wealth was no longer important to him, and he felt drawn to care for the poor.

One day, while praying before a crucifix in the chapel of St. Damien's, a local church that had fallen into disrepair, Francis heard the voice of God. "Go, Francis, and repair my house, which as you see, is falling into ruin." Frances didn't quite understand what God was talking about at the time. He thought God wanted him to repair broken-down churches like St. Damien's. Later he would realize that God was referring to rebuilding the *universal* Church.

In the meantime, with zeal in his heart, Francis went home. He took a whole bunch of expensive cloth from his father's business and sold it, together with his horse, and gave the money to the priest at St. Damien's. Francis's father could not understand his son's increasingly strange behavior, and this was the last straw. He had his son brought before the bishop to get the money back. Francis is said to have returned the money and the fine clothes off his back (literally, every last piece) to make the point that he was stripping himself of materialism and declaring his intentions of serving his *true* father, that is, his Father in Heaven.

From that point on, Francis lived a life of great poverty and rigorous fasting. (He did, by the way, clothe himself in a simple brown robe.) He fed and clothed the poor, nursed the sick, restored a few chapels, and made quite a name for himself. Several men followed his example and eventually his group became known as the Friars Minor, or Franciscans.

One day Francis was on retreat with three of his companions when a most astonishing thing happened. Francis, in his typical state of deep prayer, had a vision of a mighty angel with six wings that was nailed to a cross. Looking closer, Francis recognized the face of Jesus. He was consumed at once with joy but also with pain as he felt himself pierced in his hands, his feet, and his side. The brothers, startled by his loud cry of pain, examined these bloody wounds and were dumbfounded to see what appeared to be round black nail heads in his palms and on the tops of his feet. Even more remarkable, these "nails" seemed to pierce his hands and feet completely. Their sharp points came out the other side and were bent over backward so they couldn't be pulled out. The brothers had never seen anything like it. Francis' wounds caused him great agony and were more than his body, already broken through illness, hard work, and extreme fasting, could endure for long. Two years later, he died, and his body was laid out with the wounds visible for all to venerate. This remarkable follower of Christ was appropriately declared a saint just two years after his death.

A *Thorny* Predicament

St. Rita of Cascia lived a century after St. Francis. To please her parents, she put aside her childhood desire to become a nun and instead married a man and bore him two sons. Rita's husband treated his wife miserably throughout their marriage, but Rita responded patiently by praying for his conversion, which finally happened shortly before the man's death. After Rita's sons died unexpectedly, she found herself completely alone. She decided, therefore, to pursue a vocation as a religious sister, but this was no easy task. No one wanted her because she had been a wife and mother. Finally, the Augustinian convent in Cascia accepted the dejected widow. (It may have had something to do with the fact that their monastery doors were mysteriously unlocked one night by three heavenly visitors who came on Rita's behalf!)

As a nun, Rita showed herself to be patient, prayerful, compassionate, and holy. She spent a great deal of time meditating on the Passion of Jesus, especially on his crown of thorns. She prayed that she might take some of her Lord's suffering away. For her holy intentions, Rita received a thorn wound on the forehead. However, this would not become the object of envy and respect from the nuns in her order, for the wound gave off a most hideous odor—so unpleasant that Rita had to spend the next fifteen years in seclusion.

Many witnesses claimed to have seen a powerful light coming from this wound. And three days before her death, as Rita experienced visions of Jesus and the Blessed Mother, the rotten smell of her wound turned into the most beautiful scent of flowers, which lingered in her room long after her death.

My Heart Belongs to Jesus

St. Veronica Giuliani joined the ranks of stigmatists in the year 1697. When Veronica was only four years old, her mother became critically ill. Before she died, the woman summoned her five daughters to her bedside and with a simple prayer consecrated each of them to one of the wounds of Christ. Veronica was spiritually entrusted with the wound near Jesus' heart, which inspired her to have a great devotion to Christ's Passion. As she grew older, her father wished her to marry, but Veronica felt called to enter the convent of the Poor Clare Nuns established by our first stigmatist, St. Francis. She was seventeen years old.

Veronica turned out to be a devout and exceptional nun, and at the age of thirty-four this earned her the title of *novice mistress,* in charge of the young women who entered the order. A few years later on Good Friday, while deep in prayer, Veronica felt the crushing pains of the crown of thorns, the nails, and the lance. She had received the full stigmata. In a special way, she felt she had also been pierced in her heart.

Patiently bearing these physical sufferings, Veronica rose in virtue and holiness. Many supernatural events surrounded her, and the Church sent representatives to investigate the claims made about her. They found her to be an authentic witness of holy living. After her death in 1727, physicians examining Veronica's heart found it imprinted with pictures of the instruments used in Jesus' Passion: the nails, the crown, and the Cross. The rest of her body did not succumb to decay, but remained perfectly incorrupt (a phenomenon we'll be discussing in the next chapter). The saint's body can still be viewed at the Monastery of St. Veronica Giuliani in Citta di Castello, Italy.

Now You See It, Now You Don't

Nearly fifty years after the death of St. Veronica, a young woman named Anne Catherine Emmerich was born in western Germany, a daughter to poor farm peasants. The good and pious example of her parents helped to foster in Anne Catherine a deep love for God. From a young age she was gifted with visions of Jesus, Mary, her guardian angel, and many of the saints. She could also distinguish holy objects from unholy ones and she could correctly identify relics of the saints. Anne Catherine did not have much formal education, but somehow she was able to understand Latin perfectly the first time she attended Mass (back then, Mass was always celebrated in Latin). It was not a surprise to anyone when the young woman declared her intentions to become a nun and she entered the Augustinian Order in 1803.

Only eight years later, hard times would come upon the convent that Anne Catherine had grown to love dearly. The German territories were in a state of great turmoil, as Emperor Napoleon Bonaparte sought to control yet another European nation—and the Church. The emperor gave orders to shut down numerous religious houses throughout the area, and Anne Catherine and her community were forced to leave. With nowhere else to go, the young nun returned home.

Anne Catherine had made a visit to her parents four years earlier, during which time a most unusual thing happened. As she was praying in the local chapel before the crucifix, she asked the Lord for a share of his Passion. She knew her convent was in danger of closing, and she wanted to offer this as a sacrifice. The answer to her prayer came swiftly: terrible pains in her hands, feet, and side, although there was no visible sign of any wounds. It was the *invisible stigmata*, an equally painful suffering without any physical evidence.

But God was not planning to keep Anne Catherine's suffering a secret for long. Only a year after her convent closed, the holy nun developed the visible stigmata, including the crown of thorns, for the entire world to see. People came from all over to stare at her, but she dreaded such attention. Church officials came too, and they conducted all kinds of painful tests on the suffering woman to see if there was any hint of trickery. They could find none.

From the time Anne Catherine received the sacred wounds of Jesus until her death twelve years later, the displaced nun lived on nothing but the Eucharist—she did not take even a few drops of water! And, although she was confined to her bed for the remainder of her life due to frail health, she hardly slept at all. (We'll talk more about unusual abilities like these in chapter four.) All Anne Catherine could do during her final years of suffering was receive an endless stream of visitors. She counseled them, she identified their illnesses and prescribed remedies, she predicted future events, and she patiently put up with her visitors' admiration as well as their ridicule and suspicion.

One of Anne Catherine's visitors was a famous poet named Klemens Brantano. She recognized him immediately as the person who would help her capture her many visions on paper, since she did not have the ability to read or write. In a series of long sessions, Brantano carefully copied down all the details that Anne Catherine related from her many visions of Christ's life, Passion, and death. She demonstrated an astounding knowledge of ancient Jewish culture and geography, despite the fact that she had never left her village in Italy. Many of these details found their way into Mel Gibson's blockbuster film, *The Passion of the Christ.* Anne Catherine also claimed to have visited heaven, hell, and purgatory in her visions, and gave a detailed account of these experiences as well.

No longer wishing to be a public spectacle, Anne Catherine pleaded with the Lord to take away the visible signs of her stigmata. The wounds began to close up and disappear except for certain feast days and during Lent—particularly Good Friday—when they would bleed freely. The nun's extreme patience in suffering, her rich interior life despite her outward poverty, and her powerful example to others of living (literally) on Jesus alone, earned Anne Catherine Emmerich the title "Blessed" in the year 2004.

Two Named Therese

On Good Friday in 1898, a baby girl named Therese Neumann was born in the small town of Konnersreuth, Germany. It was a prophetic date, because Therese would experience Good Friday in a very powerful way throughout much of her life.

Therese grew into a strong young woman, accustomed to working long hours on the farm where she and her family lived. Her physical strength would be traded for a life of suffering, however, beginning in 1918 when she injured her back helping to put out a fire in one of the barns. After two hours of carrying heavy buckets of water, Therese's back gave out. A series of other injuries, including a fall down the cellar stairs in her home, left the once robust woman paralyzed, blind, and laden with a number of other ailments. Therese trusted that somehow this was all a part of God's plan, and she managed to hold firm to her faith. For strength and courage she also turned to a saint-in-the-making, her namesake Thérèse of Lisieux.

Her great faith would be rewarded. On April 29, 1923, the day Thérèse of Lisieux received the title "Blessed," Therese of Konnersreuth received her eyesight back. Two years later, when the Church made Blessed Thérèse an official saint, the bedridden Therese discovered she was no longer paralyzed. Within the following year, the other ailments that had plagued the farm woman also disappeared. But freedom from pain and suffering was not to be the final destiny for Therese. During Lent of 1926, she received the stigmata in her hands, feet, and side, followed by thorn wounds to the head and a painful shoulder lesion shortly after. On Good Friday that same year, thirty scourge marks appeared on her body. No other stigmatist in history had ever exhibited as many wounds.

Like Saint Francis, Therese's hand and foot wounds included the appearance of nails. The nail heads were rectangular in shape, slightly arched, and had defined edges. Also as with St. Francis, they appeared to penetrate through the hands and feet, with the points of the "nails" bent back against the skin on the other side. For the next thirty-six years, Therese would experience many of the mystical gifts of previous stigmatists, including living on little or no food or sleep, extensive visions, prophecy, and the ability to mystically transport to other places (another miraculous gift that will be discussed further in chapter four).

Therese Neumann died in 1962, but before she died, she would be investigated by Church officials, examined by skeptical medical and psychiatric professionals, hounded by curiosity seekers, and photographed extensively, all in an effort to determine what to do with this mysterious woman. In 2005, the bishop of Regensburg, Germany, formally initiated the process of beatification of Therese Neumann—the first step toward sainthood.

The Pierced Priest

Perhaps the most famous stigmatist of the past century was a Capuchin priest from Italy known to the world as Padre Pio. You may have seen photos of him, saying Mass with his hands bandaged and soaked with blood. He was born Francesco Forgione, son of a poor family in the small town of Pietrelcina. Little Francesco was different from his siblings and the other children of the village. He could often be found alone in prayer, deeply devoted to the Lord and his Blessed Mother. In 1902, Francesco's father entered his fifteen-year-old son in a nearby monastery to prepare him for the Order of St. Francis. A year later, the youth had received training, his habit, and the name, Brother Pio. He continued his faith journey, becoming ordained in 1910 as a Capuchin priest and taking permanent residence at Our Lady of Grace Friary in San Giovanni Rotondo in the rugged mountains of southeastern Italy.

During his religious formation, Padre (the Italian word for "Father") Pio suffered mysterious illnesses that would not respond to treatment. These included high fevers, intestinal problems, horrible headaches, and asthma. He also began to suffer from the pains of the invisible stigmata. Concerned for his health, his superiors sent Padre Pio back to Pietrelcina for a time to recover. But recovery would never be the fate of the holy priest. He continued to be plagued with physical illness in addition to mental anguish, for Padre Pio entered into battles with the devil that would leave him bruised and shaken.

On September 20, 1918, Padre Pio was praying before a large crucifix in the choir loft of the monastery at San Giovanni. Suddenly, a heavenly visitor appeared and pierced his hands, feet, and side with the visible stigmata. This would make Padre Pio the first stigmatized priest in history (Saint Francis never became a priest; he felt too unworthy of this honor and elected to remain a brother.) Padre Pio's wounds were remarkably deep, penetrating all the way through his hands and feet to the point that daylight could be seen through them, almost like looking though the hole of a donut. These wounds would bleed continuously for the next fifty years—the longest case of the stigmata on record.

The extraordinary priest from Italy was the object of much attention. People from all over the world sought him for Confession, as he was known to "read hearts" and help people with their sins. They also came in great numbers to hear him celebrate the Mass. As the time of consecration approached, the priest seemed to enter physically into the sacrifice through his sweating, heavy breathing, and pained expression. Often, as he stood at the altar, he would go into long periods of deep meditation, causing the Mass to last several hours. But the congregation wasn't the least bit bored. They loved every minute of it. The Church grew concerned that people were making Padre Pio into something of a celebrity and that he might draw attention away from Jesus. He was ordered, therefore, to stop celebrating the Mass in public, which was a great penance for the holy priest.

Padre Pio was perhaps one of the most gifted souls of all time. His list of mysterious and miraculous abilities, in addition to the stigmata, included reading hearts and souls, prophecy, visions of Jesus and Mary, daily communication with his guardian angel, being able to live on little food or sleep, miraculous healings, and bilocation (wait until you read about *that* one in chapter four!). He remained in an intense battle with the evil one until his death in 1968. Completing a long life of suffering, sacrifice, and scrutiny, Padre Pio was declared a saint in the year 2002.

A Cross in Croatia

Do stigmatists still exist today? The answer is yes. In May 1999, for example, a week after the beatification of Padre Pio, a young diocesan priest from Croatia named Father Zlatko Sudac developed a distinct mark in the shape of a cross on his forehead. Soon after, it began to bleed. The priest was sent immediately to Rome for further investigation. Those who examined the wound concluded it was not of human origin. On October 4, 2000, the Feast of St. Francis, Father Sudac received wounds in his wrists, his feet, and his side.

Before receiving the stigmata, Father Sudac had certain gifts such as speaking in tongues (a mysterious holy language), healing, and reading hearts. Since receiving his wounds, the priest has gained additional gifts, including inner conversations with Jesus, levitation, bilocation, illumination, and prophecy. Again concerned that the young priest could potentially cause a sensation and detract the faithful from keeping their hearts and minds on Jesus, the Church has currently placed Father Sudac on a remote island in Croatia where he gives retreats. Time will tell if the young priest will be another Padre Pio.

Where East Meets West

Another interesting case of the stigmata is said to be happening currently in the small neighborhood of Soufanieh in the city of Damascus, Syria. Does the name Damascus sound familiar? It should. It was the place Saul was headed when he was knocked to the ground and blinded by a vision of Jesus, leading to his radical conversion and the change of his name to Paul. In November 1982, an 18-year-old bride named Myrna Nazzour, a Christian in that predominantly Muslim country, was praying with her family and friends when she began to shiver uncontrollably. To everyone's amazement, drops of oil began to ooze from her hands. Five days later, oil was also noticed to be dripping from a small icon of the Virgin Mary kept in the family's home.

Soon after, Myrna began to have visions of Jesus and the Blessed Mother, who came, she said, to deliver messages of Christian unity. (Myrna's father is a Catholic and her mother is Greek Orthodox. The Orthodox Church split from the Catholic Church in the year 1054 and remains separated even to this day. Growing up, Myrna attended both Catholic and Orthodox schools.) In the Bible, Jesus prayed that we would be one as he and his Father are one. He did not want his followers to be divided. Myra Nazzour may end up being an important instrument to help bring Christ's separated brothers and sisters from the East and West together again. She has received at least thirty-six visions of Jesus and Mary that speak of such healing, and she has traveled extensively to bring these messages to Catholic and Orthodox parishes throughout the world. When at home in Soufanieh, Myrna and her family generously receive pilgrims of all Christian denominations as well as Muslims, who also have a devotion to the Virgin Mary. Together, they kneel side-by-side in prayer.

During her visions, Myrna is observed to perspire oil from her hands, face, neck, and eyes. Many cures have

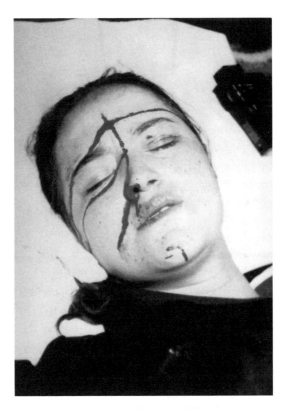

Stigmatist Myrna Nazzour of Damascus.
Photo courtesy of www.soufanieh.com.

been attributed to this oil. Even more remarkable, on Friday, November 25, 1983, signs of the stigmata became visible on the young woman's head, hands, feet, and side. Since they first appeared, Myrna's wounds have opened and bled on five Good Thursdays (the Eastern Church's term for what we call "Holy" Thursday) and closed the same day without leaving any scars. Interestingly, each of the years this has happened—1984, 1987, 1990, 2001, and 2004—are the years in which both Eastern and Western churches celebrated Easter on the same exact calendar date. During the years in-between, when this special feast has fallen on separate dates for the churches, wounds did not appear on the mystic. Perhaps these holy wounds—and their healing—will bring healing to the churches in the East and West.

✠   ✠   ✠

Since St. Francis of Assisi, more than 320 cases of the stigmata have been documented in men, women, and children. Most of these cases have involved people who are Catholic, European, and members of a religious order. However, the mystifying behavior has also been witnessed in lay people and in those of other faiths including Baptist, Anglican, and Greek Orthodox, as we've seen with Myrna Nazzour.

What are we to make of this strange phenomenon known as the stigmata? What does it mean for us individually, for our Church, and for the world? Let's begin with a word of caution. Not all examples of Christ-like wounds are considered to be authentic stigmata. We can never lose sight of the fact, for instance, that the devil is a great imitator. We're not talking about a Halloween costume devil, or the special-effects creature in a horror movie. Satan is a real and powerful fallen angel who uses all kinds of tricks to distract and confuse God's people. He can easily imitate the stigmata. Secondly, as science better understands the amazing capabilities of the human mind and body, we're beginning to realize that some individuals can create changes in their bodies—even something as bizarre as bleeding from the hands or feet—through the use of their own intense but misguided imaginations. This is what we would call "false" stigmata.

This is why the Church has to proceed carefully when it looks into these matters. Here are a few guidelines that are used to rule out non-authentic stigmata. First, the individual bearing the wounds must be humble and not flamboyant about the marks. He should not be seeking attention from others. (Remember how many saints prayed for the invisible stigmata?) Also, a person with authentic stigmata is often gifted with other supernatural abilities, but this is not always the case. As far as the wounds themselves, true stigmata are typically deep, often penetrating through the hands and feet, as in the case of St. Padre Pio. They are also very painful. They leak a significant amount of bright, red blood for days, weeks, or even years, and do not respond to medical intervention. Finally, authentic stigmata do not become infected and, with the exception of the case of St. Rita of Cascia, they do not produce an unpleasant odor. On the contrary, they can sometimes produce a most beautiful fragrance.

It's important to understand that true stigmata are not meant for a specific individual, but for the universal Church. We should be very grateful for the willingness of certain holy ones to accept and carry out such an important mission. Certainly, it is not an easy one. In addition to their physical suffering, stigmatists are often insulted, slandered, and rejected—just as Jesus was. In a sense, the stigmatist is like a living crucifix, a hard-to-ignore reminder of the powerful sacrifice God made for the children he so dearly loves. And, although it's easy to get caught up in the bloody details of the stigmata, the more important lesson here is to understand the importance and value of what suffering can mean for ourselves and others—if we accept it and use it correctly. Suffering, for example, can be a great way to grow closer to God, because it makes us more dependent on him. It can also serve as a powerful prayer that can be offered up for sins and sinners.

Still find this stuff hard to believe? Still want to stick your fingers in the wounds like St. Thomas did when Jesus appeared to his apostles after his Resurrection? That's okay. Jesus understands. And if the mere thought of such physical suffering still gives you the willies, that's okay, too. Odds are, you and I will never be asked to become heroic victims of stigmatic suffering. We don't have to look for ways to suffer beyond what God is asking of us right now. What we can and *should* do, however, is look for ways to be self-sacrificing in the little things of our ordinary daily lives. To God, these little sufferings are great gifts in themselves.

CHAPTER 3

A Well-Preserved Secret: Incorrupt Bodies

> For God created us for incorruption, and made us in
> the image of his own eternity.
>
> —Wisdom of Solomon 2:23

*A*shes to ashes, dust to dust. Although it may not be a pretty thought, one day we're all going to die. They're going to put our body in a coffin and bury it in the ground. Then, according to the laws of nature, over time our bodies will rot. First the flesh will disappear, then the bones, until eventually there's nothing left but dust. (If you opt to have your body cremated, you'll get to the same end, only faster.)

The good news, as the Bible tells us, is that at the end of time we'll get our bodies back in a glorified state. But for the purpose of this chapter, let's focus on the grim fact that after death, a buried body becomes food for worms. To avoid this process would take—well, a miracle.

We're about to embark on a discussion about a supernatural mystery known as *incorruption*. This is the rare occurrence, through the grace of God, in which certain individuals have been spared the natural process of decay. Their bodies—even hundreds of years after death—still look very much like they did on the day they died. The skin and hair are often still intact, down to the fingernails and eyelashes. The muscles are often soft and flexible and can be moved with little effort. No matter how these men, women, or children died, or how or where they were buried, their bodies remain preserved in a most extraordinary way.

Before we go any further, it's important to understand that incorruption is completely unlike any manmade attempts to preserve the body. It's nothing like the practice of mummification used by the ancient Egyptians, who discovered they could embalm bodies of their dead the same way they preserved their food—through a process of drying and salting. (Egyptians believed that the dead would need their bodies for the journey to the other world.) For despite advanced embalming techniques and fancy mummy caskets, the remains of dead Egyptians discovered by archeologists barely resemble human beings. They're so dry and brittle that just touching them could instantly crumble them to dust.

Other cultures throughout history have tried different practices for preserving their beloved dead, experimenting with varnish, honey, spices, and even rum. Even nature itself has been credited with preserving a few bodies in just the right conditions: climates that are very hot and dry or very cold and dry, or in soils containing high levels of peat, limestone, lead, or radiation. But in all of the above-mentioned cases, the preserved bodies are stiff, shriveled, dry, and downright scary-looking—not at all like the incorruptibles.

The incorruptibles we will meet in this chapter are some of the most outstanding examples. As you will discover, none of these individuals had their bodies embalmed or treated in any way after death. Many were buried in damp environments, and even though their clothing was mildewed and their caskets were rotted, their bodies were somehow unaffected. Some of them were buried without a coffin, according to the rules of their religious orders, and yet were still found in wonderful condition. A few were even miraculously preserved when found among other decaying corpses.

Since the bodies of these particular individuals did not decay, they were also spared from any noticeable stench. On the contrary, some of the incorruptibles were known to give off a sweet, lingering fragrance that could be transferred to objects that were touched to them. In other cases, oil could be found weeping from the body, often containing special healing properties. In a few cases, fresh blood has been known to flow from incorruptibles many years after their death.

Despite being handled, examined, and exposed to light, air, and temperature changes, many of these remarkable bodies are still in excellent condition even today, while others have eventually fallen prey to the natural decaying process. Sadly, a good number of incorrupt bodies were destroyed during turbulent times like the French Revolution and the Protestant Reformation. Fortunately for us, however, many of the holy bodies or parts thereof—called relics—are still safely encased in glass coffins in various churches, convents, and monasteries throughout the world. It's time to meet a few of them.

A Stiff-Necked Believer

The first known incorruptible was St. Cecilia from Rome. Cecilia was born to a wealthy noble family sometime in the second century, when persecution against Christians was common. As a child, Cecilia made a personal vow of virginity to Jesus. When her parents forced her to marry a young pagan of nobility, Cecilia informed him of her vow and told him that she was protected by an angel who accompanied her at all times. She convinced her young husband to be baptized in order to see the angel for himself. After his baptism, his eyes were indeed opened! He could see the angel, and his heart was converted soon after. His impressive spiritual growth persuaded his brother to convert, and the two young men lived out their new Christian life by serving the poor and burying the bodies of martyrs—those who had died for the Faith.

Cecilia, her husband, and her brother-in-law would eventually become martyrs themselves. The brothers were killed first, by the Romans, and Cecilia buried them with great sorrow. To kill her, the Romans locked her in the baths of her palace with the heat blasting for several days in order to suffocate her, but Cecilia did not die. Instead, she sang, which is why today she is known as the patron saint of music. Finally, an executioner was sent in to cut off her head. (I guess they'd had enough of her singing.) After three swings of his ax failed to do the job, he gave up. But the wounds would prove fatal for Cecilia. She lay bleeding on the floor of her bath for three days before death finally overtook her.

Cecilia's final act was to turn her palace and wealth over to the Pope to use as a church and to serve the poor. Cecilia was buried in the position she had died and was canonized (declared a saint) a century later. Her tomb was rediscovered in 817 and the body of the martyr was found to be incorrupt, complete with the three neck wounds. It was moved to the Church of St. Cecilia where, in 1599, the tomb was reopened with the body of the saint was still perfectly preserved. Before her tomb was sealed again, a local sculptor made a beautiful marble likeness in honor of the fallen saint.

There's an Angel on My Plow!

St. Isidore the Farmer was born around 1070 to poor but devout parents in Madrid, Spain. As a youth he went to work for a wealthy landowner, and he quickly earned his master's confidence. Isidore married a woman of great virtue who, like her husband, would also one day become a saint. Together, they had one child that, sadly, died at an early age.

Despite a life of poverty and hardship, Isidore was known to be kind to all. He generously shared his meager food with strangers, and many times it seemed that his food miraculously multiplied itself in order to feed everyone. The pious farmer never missed daily Mass, and often his deep state of prayer after the liturgy made him late returning to the fields. Some workers who were jealous of Isidore informed the landowner about this. When the landowner hid in the fields one day to investigate the situation for himself, he saw that Isidore's work was being done by invisible helpers in the young man's absence. The landowner concluded they must be angels.

Isidore passed away at the age of sixty. His body was placed directly in the earth he had tended his entire life. There was no coffin. Forty years later, his body was retrieved for a more proper burial, and the villagers were surprised to find it hadn't decayed at all. The body was moved it to the Church of St. Andrew, the first of six different relocations before it finally reached its current resting place in the Cathedral of Madrid in Spain. Wherever his body has rested, cures and miracles have been reported to take place. After eight hundred years and numerous relocations, Isidore's body has darkened and become rigid, but it is still perfectly preserved.

Who Stole My Arms?

Saint Nicholas of Tolentino (not to be confused with St. Nick of Christmas fame) was born in 1245. He recognized early in life that he had a calling to be a priest. Therefore, he entered an Augustinian monastery at a young age where he preached, cared for the sick, and spent long hours in the confessional. As an older priest, Nicholas became seriously ill. The Blessed Virgin Mary appeared at his bedside and instructed him to take a small piece of bread, dip it in water, and eat it. The ailing priest did as he was told and was cured. He, in turn, blessed bread dipped in water and distributed it to the people, curing many illnesses. St. Nicholas bread, as it has become known, is still distributed at his shrine today.

Forty years after his death, Nicholas' body was exhumed so that the Church could begin the process of canonization. The old priest's body was found to be perfectly incorrupt. By this time, incorrupt bodies were looked at as holy relics: it was not uncommon for parts of the body to be removed and sent to other locations for the faithful to venerate. At some point during the public viewing of the priest's body, his arms were mysteriously removed without permission. (Can you see the guard now: "Excuse me, where are you going with those arms?") It took a century to finally locate the arms, and quite surprisingly, even though the rest of Nicholas's boy had decomposed by that time, they were found to be incorrupt and *still bleeding fresh blood*. The sacred relics are kept in the Chapel of the Holy Arms at the Basilica of St. Nicholas in Madrid. At least twenty different times in history, they have been observed to bleed.

The Singing Monk

Blessed Peter Ghigenzi was a lawyer in Paris before he also joined the Order of St. Augustine. Because of his intelligence and excellent administrative abilities, he was soon put in charge of his order and stationed in Rome. Peter made visits to numerous religious houses and counseled his brothers spiritually. He was also known to perform many miracles.

Not long after he died in 1306, Peter's voice was heard singing along with his fellow monks as they chanted their evening prayers. Perplexed, the monks looked for the source of this singing, and discovered it was coming from Peter's tomb in the monastery. The monks obtained permission to recover their leader's remains, and to their great amazement they found Peter's incorrupt body in a kneeling position with his mouth open and his hands joined in prayer. (I'm sure their mouths must have dropped open, too!) The body was placed below the main altar of the monastery chapel where it was venerated for over six hundred years. Tragically, a fire in 1957 consumed most of building and the relic. Only a few bones were left, which are displayed each year for the faithful. It is said that, even to this day, the voice of Blessed Peter can be heard, joining his fellow monks in praising God.

A Flaky Phenomenon

Saint Agnes of Montepulciano lived at the same time as Blessed Peter, from 1268 to 1317. Agnes was a holy child who persuaded her parents to allow her to join the Dominican order when she was nine. (Nine! That's about the age when most kids are learning how to brush their teeth correctly.) It was apparent to her fellow sisters that Agnes had unusual wisdom and holiness for such a young person. She was known to fast on bread and water and sleep on the ground as penance for sin. She was also known to exhibit many of the mystical qualities that I probably don't need to tell you will be highlighted in chapter four of this book, including visions in which she held the Baby Jesus in her arms and received Holy Communion from an angel. Agnes could also levitate, multiply food, and predict future events, among other miraculous powers. At times, white cross-shaped particles fell about the young nun while in prayer. (This wasn't a bad case of dandruff or anything. It was more like the feather-light manna talked about in the bible, the heavenly food God provided for the Israelites in the dessert.)

When Agnes died, a mysterious perfumed liquid began to seep from her hands and feet, and her community took this as a sign from God that they were not to embalm her body. As if to confirm this, the body did not decay, and it was laid out in the monastery chapel for pilgrims to adore. One such pilgrim to visit the holy relic, some fifty years later, was Catherine of Siena, a saint we'll meet later in this book. Catherine had great respect for Agnes, and she approached the body reverently in order to kiss the feet of the deceased nun. Before she could do this, however, Agnes's foot rose away from Catherine, in the presence of the entire community, as if to say she did not wish to receive such reverence. Catherine gently and respectfully returned the nun's foot to its former position. She visited the body a second time, praying fervently beside it. Witnesses report that those little white particles were seen again falling down on Catherine, Agnes, and all those present.

In time, Agnes was entombed in a side wall of the main altar, and over time, helped by excessive moisture, most of her body began to decompose. The remaining incorrupt parts were encased in a likeness of Agnes and placed in the Sanctuary of St. Agnes in Montepulciano, Italy.

Raised from the Dead

Blessed Antonio Vici lived a full eighty years (1381–1461) as a holy and humble Franciscan brother. Preferring to remain a brother rather than being ordained a priest, Antonio was known as a gentle soul focused on praying, fasting, and begging alms for the poor. A year after he died, a flame was seen burning on the slab that marked his grave in the monastery floor. When the curious brothers exhumed his body, it was found perfectly preserved and sweetly perfumed. A century later, the body was retrieved a second time and still found to be incorrupt. This time it was displayed in a crystal case, and great miracles were reported soon after. For example, it is said that a knocking sound was heard immediately before the death of certain members of the religious community.

Perhaps the greatest miracle, however, occurred when a young girl thought to be possessed by the devil was brought before the holy relic in 1649. Immediately, Antonio's head, shoulders, and right hand rose several inches in the air, and the girl was cured. His posture has remained this way throughout the centuries without any support whatsoever, and no visible sign of neck ache.

Have a Seat, Sister

St. Catherine of Bologna was born to a family of wealth and nobility. Completely uninterested in the worldly lifestyle of her friends, Catherine went to Ferrara, Italy, and joined a group of Franciscan *tertiaries* (lay people who take vows of simplicity, chastity, and obedience) at the age of seventeen. She was both intelligent and mystical, producing many important writings that reflected her deep wisdom. After twenty-four years in Ferrara, Catherine was sent to the city of Bologna to establish a convent there.

When the holy nun died in 1463, her body was placed directly in the earth. Soon after, a sweet fragrance was noted at her grave, and many miracles were reported. Eighteen days later, the sisters were granted permission to retrieve the body, which they found in perfect condition. For the next twelve years, at the request of people wishing to pay their respects, the sisters would bring out the incorrupt body of Catherine on a stretcher, but this became quite cumbersome. Then they had a brainstorm: the sisters sat the body in a chair and enclosed it in a wooden case that could be wheeled out upon request.

In the year 1500, one of the nuns in the order received a vision of Catherine, in which she expressed a desire for her body to be placed in a special chapel, still in its seated position, so that the public could have access to it. This instruction was carried out immediately. A century and a half later, a grander and more ornate chapel was constructed, where the body can still be viewed today. Unfortunately, four centuries without a protective covering combined with the constant burning of votive candles and oil lamps in the chapel caused the saint's body to blacken and dry out. In 1956, a glass enclosure was constructed to protect the body from any further damage.

Earthquake Protection

Another famous incorruptible lived at the same time as St. Catherine of Bologna. Like Catherine, Blessed

Eustochia Calafato was born to nobility but had no use for it. Instead her sights were set on the Poor Clare nuns, but her father forbid her to enter this order. After his death, the determined girl pursued her dream, entering her beloved convent. After eleven years, however, Eustochia felt called to establish a new convent that followed an even stricter rule of St. Clare, which included complete poverty. Many miracles, including the stigmata, were credited to this holy nun and miracles continued after her death—not the least of which was having a perfectly flexible and incorrupt body.

In 1615, more than a century after her death, a dangerous earthquake threatened the town. After several days of tremors, the townspeople turned to the Poor Clare sisters to implore Eustochia's help and intercession. The sisters brought out the body of their foundress and sat her in her original seat in the choir stalls, where they prayed fervently. The mouth of Eustochia opened at once and her voice was heard singing the night prayer. Probably shaking more from fear than the earthquake, the nuns joined their voices with hers and the tremors soon subsided. Today, the body of Blessed Eustochia Calafato is preserved still. And although somewhat darkened over time, the wounds of the stigmata are still clearly visible.

Liquid Assets

A bit closer to our time, there are two incorruptibles worth mentioning. The first is Bernadette Soubirous, a French peasant who is arguably the most beautiful of all the holy relics. She lived from 1844 to 1879, and her story of the famous apparitions at Lourdes, France, will be told in detail in chapter five.

The second incorruptible is St. Charbel Makhlouf (1828–1898) who came from a poor but pious family

The incorrupt body of Bernadette Soubirous, visionary of Lourdes, France. Photo courtesy of the Sisters of Nevers.

in northern Lebanon. At the age of twenty-three, he became a Maronite monk and took the name of a second-century martyr, Charbel. He was ordained to the priesthood and lived a long and holy life. Charbel ate scraps and slept on the ground and was very devoted to the Eucharist. Indeed, Mass was the center of his life—when he was not preparing for it or celebrating it, he was spending time in thanksgiving for it. For the last twenty-three years of his life, he received permission to live as a hermit—a person who lives prayerfully in isolation—and that only served to amplify his wisdom and holiness.

At the age of seventy, the pious priest passed away, and according to the rules of his order, his body received neither embalming nor a casket; instead, he was buried directly in the ground. For forty-five nights after his burial, mysterious lights appeared at his grave site. Four months later, permission was granted to retrieve the body, which was found floating in the mud in its flooded grave, still perfectly intact. Once the body was washed and re-dressed and placed in the monastery chapel, it began to release a bloody sweat. The liquid was so profuse that the clothing had to be changed twice a week! Clothing that had become saturated in this unusual fluid was cut up into small pieces and distributed to the faithful, bringing relief, healing, and cures to many.

In 1927, the body of Charbel Makhlouf was sealed in a new zinc-covered coffin to protect it from the damp walls of the monastery where the tomb was located. Twenty-three years later, some pilgrims to the shrine noticed a trickle of liquid seeping from a corner of the tomb. When it was reopened, the coffin was found perfectly dry except for a small amount of fluid dripping from a crack in the foot of the casket, which had trickled its way to the outside of the tomb. The casket was opened and the body of the famed hermit was found still incorrupt and flexible, with a thick layer of fluid surrounding the body.

Word quickly spread about this wonder, and thousands of pilgrims flocked to the monastery. In just two years, over 1,200 reports of miracles were reported from contact with this fluid, including recovery from long-term illness, blindness, and even disfiguring hunchback disease. The body of St. Charbel was exhumed four times in the twentieth century, the most recent time being 1955. Although it is not known if the body is still incorrupt today, many miracles continue to be associated with this special (and somewhat soggy) saint.

✠   ✠   ✠

The subject of incorruption raises some interesting questions. First, is this peculiar form of preservation still happening today? This is a hard question to answer, because modern embalming techniques can use formaldehyde and other chemicals to interfere with the body's natural process of decay. Such interventions make it difficult to determine modern-day miracles. A perfect example of this happened recently, in 2001, when a story ran that the body of Pope John XXIII (the pope who initiated Vatican II) was found to be incorrupt thirty-eight years after his death. Later reports admitted that the intact face and body of the man (who is currently being considered for sainthood) is probably the result of a special embalming process plus three layers of caskets to prevent oxygen from destroying the body. That doesn't mean that there are no modern incorruptibles, of course, or that there aren't other authentic incorruptibles from the past that the Church has yet to discover, lying hidden away in their tombs.

The next question is why does incorruption only seem to happen to Catholics? The most logical answer to this question is that Catholics are simply on the lookout for it. The Catholic Church (along with the Orthodox Churches) has a long-standing tradition of venerating relics. That means giving their utmost respect to the bodies (or parts of bodies) of those people they consider to be holy. Since the bodies or bones of saintly individuals are seen as sacred, it is a normal process to retrieve these relics after death. In fact, one of the first things the Catholic Church does when it evaluates a person for sainthood is locate and identify his remains. This is how many incorrupt bodies have been discovered.

Here's another question: does incorruption automatically guarantee a miracle or sainthood? The answer is no. The Church considers incorruption to be a special grace or favor from God. But not every incorruptible has been named a saint. More importantly, there are plenty of well-known saints who lived a very holy life but decayed after death like most everyone else.

So, what exactly does incorruption mean to us today? Why does God grant these favors, anyway? The reasons may be as mysterious as incorruption itself, but here are a few guesses. First of all, the human body is sacred and special. Scripture tells us that the body is a temple in which God dwells. We are not just spirit; we are spirit *and* flesh. As Catholics, we believe in the promise that one day our bodies will be resurrected to join our souls in eternity. Therefore, perhaps the mystery of incorruption is meant to remind us of the holiness of the flesh today and the promise of the resurrection tomorrow.

Here's another possibility: God knows how desperately we need the example of saintly people to guide us in our own lives today. Therefore, perhaps it was his will that a few of his beloved followers would leave behind a special presence of themselves. This way, people of future generations could be reminded in a very real way that these saints truly existed. They remain close to us today, ready to help us if we call upon them. Whatever God's reasons and purposes, it's safe to say that miracles such as the incorrupt dead help the rest of us to keep our faith alive.

CHAPTER 4

Defying Logic, Reason—Even Gravity! Supernatural Saints

To one is given through the Spirit the utterance of wisdom, and to another the utterance of knowledge according to the same Spirit, to another faith by the same Spirit, to another gifts of healing by the one Spirit, to another the working of miracles, to another prophecy, to another the discernment of spirits, to another various kinds of tongues, to another the interpretation of tongues. All these are activated by one and the same Spirit, who allots to each one individually just as the Spirit chooses.

—Corinthians 12:8–11

As human beings, we are all gifted. And by gifted, I don't mean that we can play piano like Mozart, paint like Michelangelo, or dunk a basketball like Michael Jordan. Our very *existence* is a gift, and miracle. And to help enrich our existence, to help us experience the world around us,

God designed the human body with complex and marvelous abilities to see, hear, touch, taste, and smell. These five senses are fabulous gifts we should never take for granted—just ask someone who is missing one of them.

Sometimes, through the grace of God, certain people of his choosing have been known to demonstrate gifts and abilities *beyond* the five ordinary senses. It's as if the soul responds so powerfully to the love and grace of God that their "ordinary" humanness can't contain it. As a result, extraordinary things can happen. These supernatural (beyond natural) abilities are the subject of this chapter.

This Little Light of Mine: Luminosity

If you are feeling tremendously happy with yourself, your friends might say that you are positively "beaming" or "glowing." But this is just an expression. The supernatural gift of *luminosity*, on the other hand, refers to an actual light or glow in a person that can be witnessed by others. Sometimes it can appear as flames or sparks or a beam of flight projecting from a specific part of the body, such as a stigmata wound. Other times it can appear as a heavenly spotlight that seems to shine on an individual from the outside. The most common example of luminosity, however, is a glow that seems to radiate from *within* the person, surrounding his head or body in an unnatural light.

In Scripture, Peter and John accompanied Jesus to the top of Mount Tabor, where he was totally transfigured by a dazzling light. This is probably the most spectacular example of luminosity ever recorded. To a lesser degree, the face of St. Stephen, the first martyr for Christ, was seen to be literally glowing just before he was stoned to death. Throughout history, Mary, Joseph, the apostles, and other saints have often been portrayed with halos around their heads. Was this just an art style, or was it a way to capture a mysterious glow that surrounded these holy ones, as described by awed and baffled witnesses? While we're thinking about that, here are some other "shining" examples of luminosity in history.

✠ ✠ ✠

St. Ignatius of Loyola was born in northern Spain near the end of the fifteenth century. His early life consisted of gambling, women, and swordplay. However, a combat injury (courtesy of a cannonball to his legs) changed his destiny forever. During his recovery, the young man spent a great deal of time reading about Jesus and the saints, and his heart was converted. To share his enthusiasm with others, Ignatius became a priest and gifted teacher of the Faith. He founded the Society of Jesus, or Jesuits, which today is the largest religious order for men in the Catholic Church.

A famous story is told that once while celebrating Mass, Ignatius was seen to have a brilliant flame of fire hovering over his head. Thinking he might be in danger, a frightened priest assisting the Mass rushed forward to help. But when he reached Ignatius, he realized that the holy priest was in a state of deep contemplation and was completely unharmed by the flame. Talk about being on fire for God!

✠ ✠ ✠

St. Philip Neri was a contemporary and friend of St. Ignatius's. Even before becoming a priest, Philip was drawn to helping the poor and spreading the Gospel in and around Rome. At the age of twenty-nine, while praying fervently in the *catacombs*, a network of underground caves that were used to bury early Christians, he had a vision of a ball of fire entering his chest. Instantly, he felt his heart and chest become enlarged. (This, by the way, is a fact that would be physically proven after his death— doctors discovered that his rib cage was extended and his heart was twice the size of a normal heart.)

Philip founded a group of priests dedicated to preaching and teaching, called the Congregation of the Oratory. His love for God was so intense that his body produced a great heat, which required him to have his windows open all year long. At times, sparks were seen coming from the passionate priest's eyes as he celebrated Mass and preached about Jesus. He was also known to perform many miracles.

✠ ✠ ✠

Blessed Francis of Posadas was born in 1644 to very poor parents in Cordoba, Spain. He entered the priesthood at an early age and had great energy for preaching and hearing confessions. He also had a great love for the poor and the imprisoned, often giving them his own clothing to relieve their needs. Celebrating Mass was such a powerful experience for this holy young priest that he often wept through the entire liturgy (another mystical gift known as *the gift of tears*.) Sometimes a great light would be seen surrounding Francis. His skin would become as transparent as crystal and his cheeks would turn fiery red. At other times, rays of light streamed from his mouth and illuminated the missal in his hands. Twice during Pentecost, the light around Francis was so brilliant that it illuminated the whole altar!

Frequent Fliers: Levitation

To certain individuals God has granted the extraordinary ability to break the bonds of gravity and rise from the ground without any earthly support. This gift of *levitation* far surpasses the notion of "jumping for joy" or "walking on air." In true levitation, the person is so enraptured by God that he rises several inches to several feet in the air for extended periods of time, usually during great periods of deep prayer. Check out some of these "frequent fliers!"

✠ ✠ ✠

Angela Merici (1474–1540) lived in Northern Italy. She was orphaned at a young age and lost her sister soon after. During her grief, Angela was consoled by a vision (the first of many she would receive) that her sister was in heaven. Grateful for God's gift of these visions, she became a lay Franciscan and made many pilgrimages to holy places in Italy. Later in another vision, Angela was instructed to form a woman's religious order. She chose as its patron St. Ursula, an early Christian martyr and protector of women, and the order became known as the Ursulines. Many people regarded Angela as a living saint, and crowds would flock to her chapel, where she was known to levitate several inches off the floor while gazing at the Blessed Sacrament.

✠ ✠ ✠

St. Teresa of Avila was perhaps one of the greatest mystics in Church history. A Carmelite nun in sixteenth-century Avila, Spain, Teresa had a conversion of heart at the age of thirty-eight. She realized that her religious order had grown lazy, and she set about to reform it with stricter prayer, fasting, and penance. Needless to say, she was not popular with everyone! Yet despite many trials and obstacles, Teresa was successful in her reforms, and is remembered today as a *doctor*, or official teacher, of the Church.

She was also known for her many supernatural gifts, including visions, spiritual insight, the stigmata, and most especially, levitation. It was not uncommon for the young nun to elevate during Mass. Sometimes it was so obvious that her religious sisters had to literally hold her down to prevent her from disrupting the liturgy (although a bunch of nuns jumping on top of their sister like football players on a ball could be *slightly* distracting in itself!). In one of her most famous visions, Teresa saw an angel pierce her heart with a long, flaming spear. After her death, the nun's heart was examined and found to have a deep perforation that reflected this mystical experience. Her body was exhumed several times after her death and found to be sweet smelling, firm, and incorrupt. Today, Teresa's heart and other parts of her body are on display for veneration in various sites around the world.

✠   ✠   ✠

As impressive as St. Teresa's flights were, the greatest of all levitating saints was St. Joseph of Cupertino, who lived from 1603–1663. His father was a poor Italian carpenter who died before his son's birth. His mother, driven to poverty, was forced to bear her son in a stable (sound like someone else you know?). From all outward appearances, Joseph was an awkward, absent-minded, and ignorant child. No one, not even his mother, understood that he was prone to drifting into trance-like states of prayer in which he would become completely unaware of everything and everyone around him. Joseph's mother tried to enter her son in various religious orders, but no one seemed to want him. Finally, she succeeded in having him accepted into the Capuchin order, but he was dismissed after a few years because of his seeming lack of ability.

Thanks to the influence of an uncle, however, a community of Franciscans was convinced to accept Joseph as a servant. There he demonstrated great virtues such as humility, obedience, and love of penance. The Franciscans were so impressed with Joseph that they formally invited him to join their order. He was infused with spiritual knowledge (another mystical gift) and soon after was ordained a priest.

Of his many supernatural gifts, levitation was by far the most outstanding. It is said that the young Franciscan levitated almost daily at Mass. At times he would rise to the high altar where the Blessed Sacrament was kept and remain there in adoration for great lengths of time. One account has him flying from the middle of the church to the high altar, a distance of nearly forty feet! Of all his flights—they say he made more than seventy—his most famous was witnessed by Pope Urban VIII, after Joseph kissed the Holy Father's feet.

Because of the growing attention on this humble but remarkable priest, some who were jealous claimed that

St. Joseph Cupertino had the gift of levitation.

his powers came from the devil. He was brought before the *Inquisition*, a court that investigated threats to the Faith. Although Joseph was found innocent, he was kept in seclusion for the remainder of his life. His body was grounded, but his heart still soared for Jesus until his death at the age of sixty.

✠   ✠   ✠

There is one other saint worth noting when we speak about levitation. St. Mariam Baouardy was a nineteenth-century Melkite Catholic from Galilee. She was adopted by an uncle after her parents died, relocated to Egypt at the age of eight, and pledged in marriage to a Muslim man when she was thirteen. Her heart, however, was fixed on her Christian God and she refused to marry him. After that, her furious uncle beat the girl and treated her as a servant. Eventually Mariam managed to free herself from her uncle, becoming a servant for others until she entered the Carmelite order at the age of twenty-one.

There her fellow sisters quickly noted her super-natural abilities, including visions, the stigmata, and an unusual form of levitation. The "Little Arab," as she was called, could often be seen mysteriously ascending trees—not by climbing the center branches as most people would, but by gliding up the outer edges of the tree and standing on the highest, most delicate branches that would normally bend under the weight of a bird. Here at the top of these grand trees, she would sing her love for God until her superior ordered her to come down.

More Mystical Movement

In addition to being able to rise off the ground or fly across a room, certain saints and holy people have demonstrated the ability to travel mystically to far corners of the world without ever leaving their convents or monasteries. Others claim to have traveled back in history, for example, to the time of Jesus' birth or death. Still others have reported being taken to heaven, hell, or purgatory. Let's look at some examples of these mystical movers.

Blessed Anne Catherine Emmerich, the famed German visionary and stigmatic we met in chapter two, claimed that she was transported to many places through the help of her guardian angel. One of the destinations she often frequented on her mystical journeys was the Holy Land, where she witnessed details of the life and times of Jesus and the apostles. Her verbal descriptions were captured in a number of books before her death.

✠   ✠   ✠

Sister Josefa Menendez was born in Madrid, Spain in 1890. At any early age she began receiving inner *locutions*, or messages, from the Lord. At twenty-nine, she entered the Society of the Sacred Heart and soon after was invited by Christ to deliver a message of his great mercy to the world. Josefa made numerous mystical voyages to hell to witness the great suffering of the lost souls. She also suffered severe trials from the devil. Only her superiors knew about Josefa's unusual spiritual life, and they instructed her to write down her experiences. On some occasions during her visits to the underworld, Josefa would appear to be missing from the convent. Later, she could be found locked in a closet, badly beaten, her religious clothing smoking and smelling like sulfur. (And some people claim hell isn't real?)

✠   ✠   ✠

Perhaps the most sensational form of mystical move-ment is called *bilocation*, the ability to be in two places at the same time. Some saints said to have had this ability were St. Alphonsus Liguori and St. Anthony of Padua. Here are a few others that were known to be in two places at once.

St. Martin de Porres was born out of wedlock in 1579 to a Spanish nobleman and a freed black slave in Lima, Peru. He grew up in poverty, yet because of his good work with the sick and poor the Dominican Convent of the Rosary accepted him as a servant. His remarkable piety and unusual gifts led his superiors to drop the racial limits on admission to the Order, and Martin was soon made a full Dominica brother. As such Martin established a chil-dren's orphanage and hospital, and he performed sacrificial works of all kinds. He was also gifted with many abilities, including miraculous knowledge, instantaneous healings, communication with animals, and aerial flight. He was even known to bilocate. For example, although he spent his entire life at the Monastery of the Holy Rosary in Lima, witnesses claim he was seen in Mexico, China, Japan, and Africa, assisting people in prison and hospitals. To Martin, bilocation was not such a mystery. As he would point out to others, "If Jesus could multiply loaves and fishes, why can't God multiply me?" Good question, Martin!

✠   ✠   ✠

Twentieth-century visionary Adrienne Von Speyr claimed to have been directed by an angel since child-hood. Born to a Protestant family in Switzerland, she felt a special attraction toward the Catholic faith throughout her young life. Her father was more concerned with science than religion, however, and he encouraged his daughter to strive in academics. As a result, the bright young student became one of the first female physicians in her country.

Adrienne continued to develop spiritually, and as an adult she entered the Catholic Church, much to the shock and disappointment of her family. From that point on, her mystical gifts seemed to blossom, including the gift of the stigmata and increased visions. She interacted with great Catholic thinkers of her time and would write more than sixty volumes on faith and spirituality. Among her many mystical talents was her ability to bilocate. Adrienne was said to have visited Nazi concentrations camps during World War II to comfort the imprisoned, and she was also seen by witnesses in seminaries and abandoned churches.

✠ ✠ ✠

We could not talk about bilocation without mentioning Padre Pio, the famous stigmatic priest we met in chapter two. Because he lived in more recent times (1887–1968), his activities are well documented. Padre Pio was a *cloistered* Capuchin priest, meaning he almost never left his monastery in San Giovanni Rotondo, Italy. However, he was reportedly seen in many places around the world, including North America, South America, and Europe. Bishops and other credible witnesses spotted him at the Vatican on numerous occasions, at the tomb of St. Pius X in Rome at least five times, and even at the canonization of St. Thérèse of Lisieux in 1925.

Pio was a master at bilocation. To him it seemed effortless: he slipped easily into a state of sleep or unconsciousness to begin the voyage, and when it was over he had perfect recall of what happened during the journey. The humble Capuchin priest said that bilocation was simply God's way of sending him places to help others. He often appeared to people in their hospital rooms to predict their cures, or to comfort the dying. He is even said to have saved several lives during World War II: one of the most popular stories tells how Padre Pio appeared in the sky over San Giovanni Rotondo, eye-level with

Stigmatist Padre Pio of Pietrelcina. Photo courtesy of National Centre for Padre Pio, Inc.

planes, to keep them from unloading their bombs on the small Italian village. The pilots said they saw him through the windows!

Apparitions were only one way that Padre Pio could, as he put it, "prolong his personality." He could also appear in people's dreams; he could transmit his invisible presence; he could send his voice alone or he could send his entire body. Many witnesses claim to have spoken with him, and some were even able to touch him. At other times, Pio had the ability to transmit his famous *odor of sanctity*, a sweet and distinct fragrance sometimes associated with particular saints. In his case, the scent was described as a combination of flowers and tobacco.

It is said that Padre Pio was even known to be able to transport objects with him when he bilocated. On occasion he was able to bring something with him and leave it with the person he was mystically visiting; other times, he was able to take an object back with him to his monastery. He even confided to a fellow priest that at times he was able to *trilocate*—in other words, be in three places at once! Padre Pio was certainly a man who believed and demonstrated that with God, anything is possible, even if it means defying the laws of space and time.

Wonders with Words: the Gift of Tongues

The *gift of tongues* (not to be confused with the gift of gab) is another supernatural ability that can be demonstrated in several ways. For instance, it can refer to a mystical language that the angels are said to speak. (The only catch is that you need a person with the *gift of interpretation* to understand it.) The gift of tongues can include the sudden ability to speak and understand a foreign language without any prior schooling. It can also refer to a person speaking one language, yet mysteriously being understood by people of other languages. This miracle was demonstrated most famously at Pentecost, when the Holy Spirit descended upon the apostles. Afterward, they were able to go out and preach the Good News and be understood by the multitudes, despite the fact that they spoke many different languages. Finally, the gift of tongues can refer to the ability to communicate with animals. Here are a few superior speakers.

St. Anthony of Padua was born in 1195 in Lisbon, Portugal. He started out as an Augustinian monk, but later became a Franciscan friar and wound up in Padua, Italy, where he quickly rose to fame as a powerful preacher. He was a great defender of the Eucharist and his electrifying sermons drew enormous crowds wherever he spoke. It is said that all people, despite their country of origin, could understand his preaching. Anthony also drew the negative attention of non-believers. Once, frustrated by their ridicule, Anthony turned toward the sea and began to preach to the fish. The story goes that the fish surfaced and listened intently to his powerful words before submerging beneath the waves. Many non-believers (humans that is, not fish) were converted on the spot

Anthony was also known as a wonder worker for the great miracles he performed. He had visions in which he held the Infant Jesus in his arms, which is how the saint is most often represented in art. Thirty-three years after his death, the remains of Anthony were exhumed so they could be placed in a newly built church. While his body had decomposed to dust and bones, the tongue of this great preacher was found to be perfectly incorrupt. Today visitors can still see the remains of Anthony's tongue, larynx, voice box, and jaw preserved in the Basilica of St. Anthony in Padua, Italy—further witness to his heavenly gift of preaching.

✠　✠　✠

St. Francis Xavier (1506–1552) planned on being a professor in Paris until he met the famed Ignatius of Loyola. Influenced by the faith and wisdom of this future saint, Francis joined the Society of Jesus and became the first Jesuit missionary priest. For ten years, he traveled thousands of miles to India, the East Indies, and Japan. In addition to his gifts of healing, prophecy, and calming storms, Francis had a powerful gift of tongues. It played a big part of his success in baptizing over 40,000 pagans from various countries into the Catholic faith. Although he died before he could convert China, many regard Francis Xavier as the greatest missionary since St. Paul.

✠　✠　✠

Born in 1549, St. Francis Solano was a devout Spaniard who in his youth inspired many other young people. Then at the age of twenty he joined the Franciscans and, because of his ardent desire for the salvation of souls, he volunteered to evangelize the native Indians as a missionary in South America. In this new world, Francis demonstrated the gift of tongues by preaching to the tribes in their own dialect. It is said that he converted nine thousand natives during one of his homilies. Francis performed his missionary work in South America, mostly in Peru, for twenty-three years. It is believed that wild animals were subject to him, much like his predecessor and namesake, St. Francis of Assisi. Francis of Solano was also known to have the gifts of tears and levitation.

A New Lease on Life: Raising the Dead

Of all the miracles Jesus performed in the Bible, raising people from the dead was surely one of his most spectacular feats. According to Holy Scripture, Jesus brought back to life the daughter of Jairus, the son of a widow from Nain, and most notably, his good friend, Lazarus—even after he had been in the tomb for four days! The apostles of Jesus were also able to perform this powerful miracle, and as a result they made many new converts. Since biblical times, certain saints, calling upon the name of Jesus, have also been able to raise people from the dead. It is said, for example, that St. Anthony of Padua, whom we've just met in this chapter, raised *dozens* of people in this manner. Let's see who else in history was able to give people the ultimate wake-up call.

St. Patrick was born in what today is Great Britain, in the Dark Ages of the late fourth century. At the age of sixteen, he was kidnapped by Irish invaders and carried off to slavery in Ireland. There the young lad tended cattle for six years until an angel in a vision helped him to make his escape across the sea to his family. Those six years of captivity were important ones for Patrick, because he spent much of his time praying and converting his heart such that, upon his return, he decided to dedicate his life to God and enter the monastery.

Years later, when he had become a bishop, Patrick experienced a second vision in which he was instructed to return to Ireland and spread the Good News of the Gospel. He was successful as a missionary, bringing Christianity to Ireland and "driving out the snakes" (likely a symbolic term for converting the pagans, since Ireland is actually one of the few places in the world that has never had snakes slither though its grasses... makes you want to move there, doesn't it?). It is also said that Patrick had strong mystical abilities, including raising thirty-nine people from the dead.

✠   ✠   ✠

St. Hyacinth (1185–1257) was a man highly educated in law and spiritual matters. (He was probably also good at rolling with the punches, being named after a flower and all.) On a trip to Rome, he witnessed a miracle performed by St. Dominic that inspired him to become one of the first Dominicans. He was sent to reform convents in his native Poland and went on to establish several Dominican communities in Northern Europe as well as in Russia and China. Hyacinth's miracles were recorded as "countless." He seemed to have power over nature, with impressive feats such as restoring crops that were damaged by a storm and walking on water. In addition to his gifts of healing and prophecy, the Polish priest was said to have raised fifty people from the dead.

✠   ✠   ✠

St. Vincent Ferrer (1350–1419) was a Spanish-born Dominican priest who was extremely pious. To advance his spirituality, he slept on floors and fasted constantly. Vincent was a gifted preacher who delivered a powerful message of penance throughout Western Europe. He lived during the time of the *Great Schism* of the Church and labored to heal that division between East and West. (We learned a bit about that division in our discussion of modern-day stigmatist Myrna Nazzour.) Vincent is also credited with converting thousands of non-Christians in Europe. His impressive list of mystical gifts included the gift of tears and healing. Vincent is said to have raised twenty-eight people from the dead.

Chew on this: The Gift of Inedia

Most of us need a good eight hours of sleep and three square meals in order to make it through the day with a smile on our face. Many holy men and women, however, have been able to get by on far less than this because, in a sense, they have been able to "live" on God. It's important we understand that this ability is not something we can deliberately choose, even with practice. It's is a special gift and grace that God gives only to certain people—just as he has given *you* gifts and graces no one else has, even if you don't recognize them yet. The ability to survive without normal amounts of sleep or sustenance is a supernatural gift called *inedia*. Here are a few examples of saints and other holy ones who have done quite a lot on just a little.

St. Jean-Marie-Baptiste Vianney (1786–1859) was the son of a poor French farmer. Poorly educated, Jean-Marie had a difficult time pursuing his dream of entering the religious life. He finally passed the exams for ordination and was made a priest at the age of thirty, but his teachers and peers regarded him as a real dunce. Accordingly, for his assignment he was sent to the remote village of Ars, France, for the remainder of his life. There Jean-Marie began to exhibit extraordinary abilities. He ate simple foods and slept on a hard bed only two hours a night, during which time he claimed he was often attacked by the devil. His most prominent gift was the ability to read the hearts and minds of those who came to make a confession. Because of this, he rapidly earned great respect as a confessor and attracted people from far and wide to the little town of Ars. It is said that the holy priest spent thirteen to seventeen hours a day in the confessional. Not surprisingly, he is the patron saint of priests. Not bad for a guy who could barely make priesthood himself!

✠ ✠ ✠

St. John Bosco (1815–1888) discovered God's will for his life through a series of vivid dreams. (No, one was not to invent a yummy chocolate ice-cream topping.) In the first dream, young Bosco was told that he would eventually lead badly behaved boys through his example of gentleness and kindness. As he grew in age and holiness, John was ordained a priest. On one occasion he witnessed the sad fate of street children who had landed themselves in prison, and he vowed that he would dedicate the rest of his life to rescuing these unfortunate youngsters. He began to take boys in and educate them in academics and spiritual matters. In time, he founded the Salesians, a religious order named after St. Frances de Sales, to help him carry out his work in Italy and other countries around the world. John displayed many supernatural gifts, including luminosity, levitation, and the multiplication of food. Although he was large in stature, he barely ate or slept. Still, before he died he mustered enough energy to establish and oversee 250 Salesian houses to assist some 130,000 children.

✠ ✠ ✠

St. Maximilian Kolbe was born at the very end of the nineteenth century, the rather undisciplined son of a poor Catholic family in Poland. When he was the age of twelve, things changed when he had a vision of the Virgin Mary offering him two crowns. One, she told him, was white for purity; the other was red for martyrdom. Young Kolbe chose both. From that point on, he turned his attention to Christ and the Blessed Mother, eventually becoming a Franciscan priest. Although a bout with tuberculosis left him in frail health for the rest of his life, the passionate young priest started a magazine to stir up religious zeal in his Communist-suppressed country. He also established a new monastery, and was known to possess spiritual gifts such as luminosity and the reading of hearts.

When the Nazis invaded Poland some years later, Kolbe's religious house was closed, the presses were shut down, and the Franciscan was sent to prison. There, despite his frail health, he ministered tirelessly to prisoners. Kolbe met his end when the Nazi guards decided to execute ten prisoners in reprisal for an escape, and he volunteered to die in place of a married man who had three young children. His offer was accepted and he was locked in a room without food or water. The only sustenance he had was the bread and wine smuggled to him for the secret celebration of the Mass. Kolbe survived on this holy meal alone, until death finally claimed him fourteen days later.

You Shall Not Live on Bread Alone
(Except for this Kind)

Maximilian Kolbe brings up another even more fascinating form of *inedia*—the ability to survive on the Eucharist alone. Here are three examples of why the Eucharist is called the Bread of Life...

St. Catherine of Siena (1347–1380) was the twenty-third of twenty-five children. (Can you imagine the line for the bathroom?) Devout and wise beyond her years, she experienced visions as early as the age of six, and went on to become a Third Order Dominican—a group of lay people dedicated to serving Christ in the secular world. She was perhaps one of the greatest female mystics in history, with powerful abilities to heal, levitate, and expel demons. She also bore the stigmata (invisible, at her request) and received extensive visions and dictations from Jesus.

St. Catherine of Siena is regarded as one of the greatest mystic saints in history. (St. Catherine of Siena by Domenico Beccafumi, Wikimedia Commons.)

Catherine was one of the few saints to be "mystically married" to her Savior. What she saw as a beautiful ring of gems on her finger that she said was given to her by Christ, others could only see as a ring of swollen flesh.

Despite her lofty visions, however, Catherine had her feet planted firmly on the ground. She worked diligently for Church unity, even persuading Pope Gregory XI to return from Avignon, France, to his rightful post in Rome. Toward the last part of her life, Catherine received a vision in which she was able to drink the blood of Jesus that came from the wound in his side. (I know that sounds rather vampirish, but think of it more like the ultimate Holy Communion.) After that experience, she lived on nothing but the Eucharist for the remaining eight years of her life. She died, like Jesus, at the age of thirty-three.

✠   ✠   ✠

Nicholas of Flue (1417–1487) was born in Switzerland and was spiritually advanced from the time he was a child. He eventually married and had ten children. After twenty-five years of marriage, Nicholas was given permission from his holy wife to leave his family and live as a hermit in order to pursue a deeper spirituality.

Shortly after he had retired to a life of isolation in a cave, Nicholas began to suffer severe stomach spasms to the point where he was sure he would die. When the pain eventually left him, so did his appetite for all food or drink. He survived on nothing but the monthly Eucharist for twenty years, during which time people from all walks of life sought the holy hermit for advice and counsel. So much for living alone!

✠   ✠   ✠

Therese Neumann, the German stigmatist we met in chapter two, lived a highly mystical life for many years. It is estimated that she suffered the entire Passion mystery some 750 times. No wonder she was the most supernaturally marked person in history, bearing nine thorn marks in her head, a shoulder wound, thirty scourge marks, and a face often covered by tears of blood. Therese's stigmata lasted thirty-six years, second only to that St. Padre Pio, who bore his wounds for fifty years. It is said that Therese lived on the Eucharist alone for thirty-five years until her death.

✠ ✠ ✠

We've certainly covered a number of supernatural abilities in this chapter. We've met saints and other holy people who could float in the air, glow in the dark, raise people from the dead, heal the sick, predict future events, and live on the Eucharist alone, just to name a few. Many of the people we've just read about could actually do several of these things. Talk about multi-tasking!

So what are we supposed to make of all of this? The Church looks upon physical displays of wonder with great caution. In its wisdom, the Church understands that bizarre behaviors can also be the result of an unstable individual or the work of the great imitator, the devil. The Church is not in a position to authenticate specific abilities; it simply looks to see if a supernatural element is involved. What's more important for the Church than any physical sign is the character and growth of the individual. Is the person of sound mind? Is he craving attention or acting in an unbecoming way? Or is the individual humble about his abilities and concerned only about growing closer to God?

To be authentic, special talents like the kind discussed in this chapter should be a bi-product of a person's holiness, not the main event. *Jesus* is the main event. We must never let signs—no matter how wonderful—distract us from that truth. The other important point to keep in mind here is that physical signs are not necessary for a person to be considered a saint. The far majority of saints had no supernatural qualities whatsoever. Heroic virtue, especially in the face of difficulty, is far more important in distinguishing true servants of God.

More important than the question of *how* supernatural events happen is that of *why* they happen. And why don't they happen to more of us! Perhaps we can think of it this way: God's grace is all around us. It's abundant, it's marvelous, and it's there for everyone. Since our God is a generous God, he has no favorites. We are all his beloved children. The difference between you and me and the mystics mentioned in this chapter is not that we've been created any differently than they were. The mystic has simply been graced by God in this special way and has developed an advanced way of responding to that grace.

Here's a visual for you. At one time, almost every rooftop in America sported a big, ugly TV antenna so that people in the house could watch just a few channels of television. Today, these wire monuments have been replaced with underground cables and in some cases slick little satellite dishes that can receive a jillion stations in perfect clarity. The broadcasters haven't fundamentally changed, but the receptors have, and that makes all the difference.

We, like the saints, are invited to improve our reception to God's graces and be more "tuned in" to what his will is for us. Then we can become powerful instruments of grace, like the people we've just read about in this chapter. How do we do this? The answer is through prayer, spiritual reading, and the sacraments —especially the Eucharist and Confession. Now, please don't misunderstand me. Just because you start reading your Bible or attend Mass a bit more often doesn't mean you're going to start flying around your bedroom tomorrow. As the Scripture quote at the beginning of this chapter says (and I *know* you've read it) gifts are given as the Spirit chooses. But what I can assure you is that prayer, spiritual reading, and the sacraments won't disappoint. They are the true source of fulfillment and happiness, and what greater spiritual gift is there than that?

Chapter 5

Visions, Visitors, and Voices: Apparitions

A great portent appeared in heaven: a woman clothed
with the sun, with the moon under her feet, and on
her head a crown of twelve stars.

—Revelation 12:1

In the last chapter we learned about some pretty amazing supernatural gifts. One of these, the gift of receiving visions, is so important it deserves a chapter of its
own. First, let's clarify what we mean by visions, or *apparitions*. You may hear this word used in non-religious con-
texts when talking about ghosts. But ghosts, for the most
part, refer to a separate a category of spirits: those who
can't seem to leave the earth because they have unfin-
ished business to do. They are often noisy and pesky and
inconvenient.

We're not talking about ghosts here. What we want
to focus on in this chapter are the times in history when

God has chosen certain people to see or hear something important, something that he wishes to reveal to the rest of the world.

For the purpose of clarification, there are three main kinds of visions. The first kind is perceived by a person's physical eyes and ears, the organs we normally use to perceive the world around us, although the visionary is the only one able to see and hear it. The second and most common type of vision is perceived with the imagination in a dream state or a deep trance. The seer "sees" and "hears" it, even if his eyes are closed. The third and most unusual kind of vision does not involve words or pictures, but is understood with the mind alone. A person experiencing this kind of vision usually has difficulty afterward describing it in human terms. Some people have said it's like being swept up suddenly and placed before the very throne of God.

Under the Watchful Eyes of the Church

Although visions or apparitions may be new to you, they are certainly not new to history. God has used visions of all types to communicate with his people since early biblical times. Heavenly messengers, for example, appeared to Abraham and Sarah to tell them they would have a son in their old age; to the shepherds at Bethlehem to announce the birth of the Savior; and to Joseph and Mary, warning the couple to flee to Egypt to escape Herod's great wrath.

The fact that visions continue to be reported today should not surprise us. However, we need to approach them (as we do all claims of the supernatural) with a good deal of caution. As we've already been reading, the devil is a crafty enemy. He's been known to confuse and mislead people through visions. As St. Paul warns in Scripture, he can even appear himself as an "angel of light." St. Martin of Tours, a bishop from the fourth century, can certainly attest to that. He had a vision of a young man in royal garments, surrounded by a dazzling light, announcing he was Christ returning. Martin wisely told the vision, "The Lord Jesus did not say he would return in purple with a crown. I will not recognize my Savior unless I see him as he suffered, with the stigmata and the Cross." The apparition immediately vanished.

To help guide and protect its flock in the area of apparitions, the Catholic Church makes an important distinction between what it calls *public* revelation and *private* revelation. Public revelation refers to the ways God has revealed himself in word and action, particularly through the person of Jesus Christ—revelations that have been handed down through the Bible and the Church's Sacred Tradition. These revelations are for all people, for all times. Public revelation came to an end with the death of the last apostle. (By the way, St. John was the last apostle—he was not martyred like the others, but lived to a ripe old age in modern day Turkey, where he wrote parts of the New Testament.) As Catholics, we are required to believe in public revelation. It's critical to our faith.

At the same time, the Church doesn't want to put God in a box and limit his creativity. The Church recognizes that God can and does continue to make himself known to his people. He may use visions and messages, for example, to help his children survive particularly challenging times in history. These post-biblical encounters are called private revelation. Unlike public revelation, *Catholics are not required to believe in private revelation.* These types of visions are only binding to those who see and hear them. Still, the Church understands that private revelation can sometimes be helpful for our spiritual growth. Therefore, it looks carefully at reports of visions to sort out which apparitions are worthy of our belief and which ones aren't. How does it do this? First, it takes into consideration the credibility of the seer. Second, it looks at the messages themselves to make sure they do not contradict the Bible in any way, or add anything new to the Faith. And third, it makes sure that the apparitions are bearing good fruit: bringing people closer to Jesus, to the Gospel, and to the sacraments.

Visions of the Virgin

What exactly do people see when they experience visions? Some seers claim to see and hear from Jesus. Others describe personal visits from angels or a particular saint. But the most common heavenly visitor reported is the Blessed Virgin Mary. Interestingly, there has been a dramatic increase of Marian apparitions in recent times. In fact, more visions of Mary have been reported in the last two centuries than all other centuries combined, and the number continues to escalate around the world. Why the sudden and unprecedented increase? And why the emphasis on Mary? Perhaps we are living in one of those challenging times in history when God wants us to know that he's there for us. Perhaps he uses his Mother, since she is the one who always points to her Son, because we need to be pointed to him now more than ever. Maybe he simply hopes that his children—even those with the hardest of hearts—might still have a soft spot for Mom.

The messages themselves may also hold a clue about why there seem to be so many apparitions. Over the past century or two, there seems to be a common theme: God is offended by the sins of the world; people are urged to increase their prayer and sacrifices and return to the sacraments; and great punishments are headed our way if things don't change pretty soon. This sounds rather important, like we ought to be paying attention!

Visions can be a brief, one-time event, or something that lasts for decades. They can be private, known to only a small group of people, or they can be world-famous. Here is just a brief sampling of some of the most well known visions in history that the Church has found worthy of our belief. I think you'll find them quite eye-opening.

Millions Converted in Mexico

Mexico in the 1500's was suffering at the hands of the Aztecs, a bloodthirsty culture that sacrificed some 50,000 men, women, and children each year to its various gods. When the Spanish invaded the country, Franciscan missionaries followed close behind to spread the gospel to the natives. Many were baptized. One winter morning in 1531, a newly baptized peasant named Juan Diego was walking to Mass. As he crossed Tepeyac Hill, the site of a former shrine to the pagan goddess of the earth that lay on the outskirts of what is now Mexico City, he was stopped by a vision of the Virgin Mary. Appearing as a pregnant peasant girl, she asked Juan to tell the bishop that she desired a sacred place to be built on this hill so she could pour out her grace on all those who called upon her. The bishop, not believing the story, asked for a sign to prove what Juan was telling him was true.

The next day, Juan returned to the hill and suggested that the Virgin choose a better messenger than himself, but she simply instructed him to ask again. Once more the bishop demanded a sign. On the third day, Juan tried to avoid meeting the Virgin by choosing a different path, but she appeared to him anyway. (Like we can really pull one over on the Blessed Mother!) She told Juan to climb the hill and gather roses that were growing there, although it was wintertime. This would be a sign for the bishop. Juan gathered the roses, and the Virgin arranged them carefully in his woven cloak or *tilma* and sent him on his way. When he opened his cloak in front of the bishop and let the roses fall out, all onlookers were amazed—not at the out-of-season flowers, but at an image of the Virgin that had been mysteriously imprinted on the inside of the cloak. The bishop fell to his knees, begging Mary's forgiveness for his unbelief. Immediately, he set about plans to construct the sanctuary.

News of the apparitions and the mysterious image spread quickly throughout the land. In the following seven years, more than eight million native Mexicans were converted to Catholicism and the Aztecs were forced to stop their human sacrifice. This victory over bloodshed—and the fact that the Virgin appeared to Juan Diego as pregnant with the Christ Child—is the reason this particular Marian image has become a symbol for the pro-life movement. Today, the miraculous image on Juan Diego's cloak is still on display at the Basilica of Our Lady of Guadalupe in Mexico City, one of the most popular Catholic shrines in the world.

Over the past century, many scientific tests have been conducted on the *tilma* of Guadalupe, but they seem to reveal more mysteries than answers. For starters, the fact that the *tilma* has remained intact for over 400 years is unexplainable. The coarse cloak, made out of cactus fibers, should realistically have a life expectancy of thirty or forty years before decomposing. Yet Juan Diego's *tilma* remains intact despite the fact that it was unprotected from the air, elements, and veneration of the faithful for the first hundred years after the miracle.

Even encased in glass as it has been over the past few centuries, the image should have been expected to fade in the humid, salty environment of Mexico City. Yet on the contrary, the colors—many of which seem to be non-reproducible by contemporary artists—remain as vivid today as they were 400 years ago. Infrared radiation photography confirms there is no evidence of paint or brush strokes, corrections, underlying sketches, or varnish on the cloth. How the image was placed on the cloak remains a mystery. And secrets continue to unfold. Close-up digital images of the Virgin's eyes, for example, reveal startling reflections of Juan Diego, his family, and his bishop—those who were present in the room when the image was revealed.

Not surprisingly, even today the miraculous image of Guadalupe continues to convert people to the Faith.

The Miraculous Medal

It was 1830 and Paris was in a great state of turbulence. The French Revolution a few decades prior had brought radical changes in government, military, industry, and above all, religion. France, which had long been known as a strong Catholic country spawning saints, popes, and mystics, now found itself caught up in the "Age of Enlightenment," in which people focused on their wonderful knowledge and cleverness and forgot all about God. Practicing religion had become not only unpopular, but also dangerous. (Doesn't sound very enlightened at all, does it?)

In these difficult times for the Church, a young Parisian nun named Catherine Labouré of the Daughters of Charity began to have visions of the Virgin Mary at her convent, located on a famous street called *rue du Bac*. The first vision took place on the night of July 18, 1830, when an angelic child woke Catherine and invited her to come to the chapel. There, Catherine saw the Virgin Mary sitting in the chair reserved for the spiritual director of the order. As Catherine approached the chair in reverence, the Virgin told her that she had a special mission for her. Bad times were about to befall Paris and all of France. She spoke of the throne being toppled, priests and religious being persecuted, and blood flowing in the streets of Paris. Pointing toward the altar, the Virgin told Catherine that it was the source of all consolation.

A week after the apparitions, bloody riots broke out in Paris, just as the Virgin had predicted. These would be followed by other such uprisings throughout France. Four months later, while praying with her community, Catherine saw the Virgin a second time. This time she appeared standing on a globe with a golden ball in her hands. Her fingers were covered with rings that produced dazzling rays of light. Through an interior voice, Catherine learned that the ball represented the world and that the rays of light symbolized the graces the Virgin

The incorrupt body of St. Catherine Laboure, visionary of the Miraculous Medal. Photo courtesy of the Central Association of the Miraculous Medal.

promised to shower on all who asked for them. Surrounding this vision was an oval frame with the words, "O, Mary, conceived without sin, pray for us who have recourse to thee." Catherine was instructed to have a medal created of this image. The Virgin promised great graces and special favors for those who wore the medal confidently around their neck.

A month later, Catherine would have a similar vision of the Virgin, with the same request for a medal. The young nun confided in her spiritual director about the visions, and after careful discernment he received permission from the archbishop of Paris to have the medal struck. It wasn't long before millions of medals were distributed throughout France and Europe, and with them came a renewed devotion to Catholicism and the Virgin Mary. The medal has become known as the "Miraculous Medal" for the graces and miracles it has been known to obtain for its wearers.

Cures Spring up in Southern France

On the heels of the apparitions at *rue du Bac* came another important series of visions in France. This time they occurred in the small mountain village of Lourdes, near the border of France and Spain. Although located far from the city of Paris, rural areas like Lourdes were not exempt from the devastating effects of the French Revolution. Many people were without work, disease was rampant, and the Church was continuing to feel the pressures and persecutions of secular thinking.

Beginning on February 11, 1858, a poor and sickly child named Bernadette Soubirous experienced eighteen visions of the most beautiful young lady she had ever seen, in an abandoned grotto outside of her town. The lady wore a long white dress with a blue sash, with golden roses on each foot. In her hands was a large set of rosary beads. During the first two apparitions, the lady smiled but was silent as Bernadette prayed the rosary before her. At the third apparition, however, she began to speak, and invited Bernadette to come to the grotto for fifteen days. She also told the child that she could not promise her happiness in this world, but in the "other"; meaning that by living an earthly life close to Jesus, Bernadette could be assured of happiness one day in heaven.

In the next several appearances, Bernadette would learn that she, like Catherine, had been entrusted with a special mission: to pray and perform acts of penance (or sacrifice) for sinners. One of these acts was to crawl on her knees in the mud of the grotto and kiss the ground. Bernadette did not wonder to herself who the wonderful lady was, although the townspeople were convinced it was the Virgin Mary. Her only concern was to please the beautiful lady. Therefore, she carried out every task obediently, even when she was told by the lady to wash herself and drink from a spring that didn't seem to exist. After digging in the dirt where the lady had pointed, however, she was eventually able to find some muddy water from which to drink and to wash. This water soon began to flow strong and clear and, even more miraculously, it seemed to bring healing to people with illness and disabilities. (Thank goodness Bernadette, unlike most kids, listened to her mother when she was told to wash!)

The lady also asked Bernadette to tell the priests to have a chapel built at the grotto and to invite people to come in procession. The priests at first were skeptical, until Bernadette finally succeeded in getting the lady's name. "I am the *Immaculate Conception,*" the lady told her. This term, which means "conceived without the stain of Original Sin," was a title the Church had formally recognized for the Blessed Mother only four years before. It was so new there was no way an uneducated peasant

St. Bernadette Soubirous, the visionary of Lourdes, France. Photo © Leonard von Matt.

child like Bernadette could have made it up. Convinced that these visions were genuine, the bishop approved the apparitions and had a magnificent sanctuary built above the grotto at Lourdes.

For the past 150 years, millions have visited the shrine at Lourdes to drink, wash, or bathe in the miraculous waters of the spring. Numerous cases of physical cures have been documented by the Church, including cures of paralysis, blindness, tuberculosis, chronic gastroenteritis, and cancer. But physical cures are not the only miracles that take place in Lourdes. Large numbers have claimed to be healed of emotional and psychological maladies such as addiction, depression, and mental illness. Perhaps the greatest miracle of Lourdes, however, is the spiritual conversions that enable pilgrims to turn their lives over to God and unite their sufferings with his.

Knock, Knock, Who's There?

Ireland in the 1800s had its own share of problems. The Irish people were under the oppressive rule of England. Times were tough, particularly for Catholics, who were not allowed to vote, own land, or carry a sword. To make matters worse, a great potato famine struck in the mid-1800s, leading to the deaths of 1.5 million Irish. An additional million were forced to leave their native land in search of a better life in America or Canada.

On August 21, 1897, in the small village of Knock on the west coast of Ireland, a ray of hope appeared for the downtrodden people. Fifteen parishioners between the ages of five and seventy-five witnessed an extraordinary illuminated scene on the exterior wall of the parish church. The figures in the scene included the Virgin Mary, St. Joseph, and the apostle, St. John. The Virgin was dressed in white garments, with a brilliant crown on her head and her hands raised in prayer. On her right stood St. Joseph, also in white, with his head tilted respectfully toward his spouse. On her left stood St. John, dressed as a bishop, with an open book in his hand. He appeared to be preaching. Behind them and to the left of St. John was an altar decorated with a lamb and a cross, surrounded by angels.

The witnesses who saw this apparition stood in the pouring rain for two hours, quietly reciting the rosary, their eyes glued to the spectacular sight before them. While they were drenched from the rain, the ground underneath the illuminated figures and the exterior wall of the church remained perfectly dry until the apparition ended. There were no messages associated with the apparition at Knock, but this special one-time vision did much to strengthen a diminishing faith in Irish Catholics.

Great Balls of Fire!

Emperor Napoleon of France invaded many European nations in the 1800s, including the little country of Portugal. Even after the invaders were chased out at the turn of the century with the help of Britain, Portugal had difficulty recovering from the attack. A corrupt king and an economic crisis further troubled the people. The First Republic, a new form of government, was established in 1910, but it did little to solve the country's growing problems. What's more, the new government resented the influence of the Catholic Church and did what it could to stifle it.

Shortly thereafter, much of Europe became ensnared in the great global conflict that was World War I. It was during this turbulent time for all humankind that one of the most important apparitions in Church history took place, in the small village of Fatima, Portugal. In the year

1916, three shepherd children, Francisco (age nine), his sister Jacinta (age seven), and their cousin, Lucia (age ten) had three mystical encounters with an angelic figure. The angel taught them special prayers, gave them Holy Communion, and asked them to make sacrifices because the world had greatly offended God with its sins. The children told no one about these mysterious visits.

Then, on May 13, 1917, while in a field with their sheep, the three children saw two bright flashes of light. Thinking it was lightning, they turned to leave. That was when they spotted a beautiful lady, hovering above a small tree in the field. She was clothed in white and radiated a most brilliant light. She told the children she had come from heaven and asked them to come to the field on the thirteenth day of each month at the same hour. She also asked them to bear many sufferings that God would send them, and the children agreed.

The lady kept her word and returned on the thirteenth of each month. Jacinta could no longer contain herself and confided to her parents about the apparitions. Word spread rapidly throughout the village and crowds began to gather at the field, even though it was dangerous because of the anti-Catholic government. Each month, the lady gave important and specific messages to the children. She asked them to recite the rosary every day to bring an end to the war and peace to the world. She also asked them to make sacrifices for sinners and even showed them a terrible vision of hell.

In addition, the lady predicted many things about the future. She said the Great War would end, but that a more terrible one would begin if people did not change their hearts. The world would know this new war was upon them because of a sign that would appear in the sky. She also predicted that Russia—which that very year

The three visionaries of Fatima, Portugal. Jacinta and Francisco Marto, and Lucia dos Santos. Photo courtesy of the Sanctuary of Fatima.

was undergoing its Communist revolution—would spread its evil ways throughout the world and that many people would die unless that nation was consecrated to her Immaculate Heart.

The lady also gave the children private messages, which they were to keep secret. She told Lucia, for example, that her cousins would go to heaven soon, but that Lucia would remain on earth a long time to fulfill Jesus' mission. Finally, the lady promised to reveal her identity in October, when she also promised to perform a miracle unlike any seen before.

October 13 brought heavy rainfall. It drenched the crowd of 70,000 that waited anxiously in the field for hours in anticipation of the great miracle. When the lady appeared, she told the children that she was Our Lady of the Rosary. Then she rose into the sky and extended her hands. An enormous ray of light came out from her hands and parted the clouds to make the sun appear. As she neared the sun, the children could also see St. Joseph with the Child Jesus.

Although the crowds could not see any of this, they did see what happened next. Reports say that the sun began to spin and shake. Everyone present could look upon it without blinking or squinting. The sun then began to dance, turning different colors and sending bright rays of color to the earth below. Amazed, the people fell to their knees. Suddenly, the sun left its place in the sky and seemed to race toward the earth as a ball of fire, causing terror among the people, before it ascended and continued its spectacular light show. When the Miracle of the Sun was over, the crowds—half terrified and half thrilled—realized that their clothes were completely dry. It was indeed a miracle.

The apparitions at Fatima are important not only because of the great miracle, but because of many predictions that have come true. As the lady foretold, Francesco and Jacinta died a few years after the apparitions, while Lucia became a Carmelite nun and lived for ninety-seven years. Russia, as predicted, became a great power, spreading the evil of Communism throughout Europe and persecuting the Church. And a second and more terrible war indeed followed, preceded by an eerie green light that appeared in the sky throughout Europe. Scientists would call it an unusual display of Northern Lights, but believers remembered the Virgin's prophecy about the sign in the sky. Russia would not begin to lose its stranglehold on Eastern Europe until the early 1980s, when a Polish pope named John Paul II emerged as a challenge to its decades-long persecution of believers. Shortly after, the walls of Berlin—and Soviet Communism—came tumbling down. Pope John Paul II had a special place in his heart for the Fatima apparitions. He believed the Blessed Mother had protected his life in 1981 when he was shot by an assassin—on May 13, feast day of Our Lady of Fatima.

Apparitions in Amsterdam

It was during World War II that another set of prophetic apparitions took place, this time in the city of Amsterdam in the Netherlands. Much of Europe was in ruins from the war and the future looked grim. Amsterdam itself was being occupied by Nazi soldiers. It was then, beginning on March 25, 1945, that Ida Peerdeman, a forty-year-old humble and devout Dutch woman, began to have visions of the Blessed Mother and receive urgent messages about the state of the world and events to come. The apparitions would continue until May 31, 1959.

Giving herself the title, "The Lady of All Nations," the Mother of God told Ida that she had been sent to tell the world to put the cross of her Son back at the center of everything, or there would be no peace. She made many serious predictions about the future and emphasized the importance of the Eucharist, which she referred to as the "Daily Miracle." Amsterdam was chosen as the place to reveal her messages, she said, because of the great Eucharistic Miracles that had taken place there long ago. (If you forgot which ones they were, you'll find them in chapter one!)

In addition to the messages, the Lady showed Ida a special image she wished to spread throughout the world, just as she had done with Catherine Labouré. As in Catherine's vision, the image shown to Ida had the Blessed Mother standing on a globe with her hands outstretched and rays of light shining from them. This time, however, she was standing directly in front of a cross, which was firmly implanted in the earth. The words, "The Lady of All Nations" encircled her head. She also gave Ida the following prayer, requesting that the world pray it daily:

> Lord Jesus Christ, Son of the Father, send now
> Your Spirit over the earth.
> Let the Holy Spirit live in the hearts of all nations
> that they may be preserved from degeneration,
> disaster, and war.
> May the Lady of All Nations, who once was Mary,
> be our Advocate. Amen!

There was something else special about the apparitions in Amsterdam. The Lady requested that the Church formally make it known to the world that she is Co-*Redemptrix*, *Mediatrix*, and *Advocate*. These words may sound confusing, but their meaning is fairly simple. As we know, Jesus came into the world, sent by the Father, to save us from sin. He could have come into the world in many ways —he could have hatched from an egg or flew in on a spaceship—but God willed it that Jesus would come into the world like we all did, through a mother.

But not just any mother: the one woman who from all people and all eternity was selected for that special job! Because Mary gave Jesus flesh (his divinity came from the Father) and because she suffered along with her Son, we can say she has played a uniquely important part in the redemption of humanity. Hence the title, Co-Redemptrix.

We also remember that before he died, Jesus gave his mother to the world saying, "Behold your mother." From that point on, Mary became mother of us all, or, you could say, the Lady of All Nations. Together with her children, she calls down the Holy Spirit to help save the world from evil and disaster. This is where the names Mediatrix and Advocate come in: Mary has a unique and powerful place as an *intercessor* before the power of God. To this date, although the Church has recognized Mary's special role in redemption and salvation for centuries, it has not yet declared a formal teaching, or *dogma*, about these titles.

The bishop of Amsterdam conducted an investigation while Ida was still having her apparitions, but he could not find enough evidence to conclude that it was a supernatural matter. He found the predictions of the Lady unclear and even frightening, and did not feel that the apparitions were worthy of belief. Forty years later, however, after many of the predictions had come true, Bishop Henry Bomers came to a different conclusion. He declared that the public could now venerate the title and image of the Lady of All Nations, and pray the prayer given to Ida. As far as the specific messages that were recorded by Ida Peerdeman, people were permitted to decide for themselves whether or not to believe them. Ida lived long enough to see the bishop's approval, just as the Lady had predicted. Jozef Marianus Punt, the succeeding bishop, took the matter one step forward. In 2002, he declared that the phenomena of Amsterdam were indeed supernatural.

It's a Bird, It's a Plane...

We often think of the 1960s as a time of cultural revolution in our own country, but in fact there was turbulence going on then in many parts of the world. Egypt was no exception. In 1966, the Egyptian government banded with other Arab countries to attack its neighboring enemy, Israel, in a famous war that Israel would win in only six days. A small portion of the population of Egypt consisted of Coptic Christians, both Catholic and

The glowing figure of a lady atop a Coptic Catholic Church in Egypt was witnessed by millions in the course of three years. Photo courtesy of www.zeitun-eg.org.

Orthodox, and these people in particular suffered the economic pressures and discrimination of their government. Many fled Egypt, seeking better opportunities in the Western world.

Just outside of the capital city of Cairo is a small suburb known as Zeitoun. (*Zeitoun*, by the way, is the Egyptian word for olive, a traditional symbol of peace.) It is widely believed that the Holy Family rested in this place during their flight to Egypt, but on April 2, 1968, the town became famous for another reason. That warm spring evening, Muslim workers in a garage across the street from a Coptic Orthodox Church were startled at the sight of a young lady in white walking around the domes on top of the church. Looking closer, they realized that the lady was actually *floating*. She wore a glittering crown and was surrounded in light: it was the Virgin Mary, a woman highly respected by Muslims as one chosen by God to be the mother of the prophet, Jesus. The apparition lasted for two hours, drawing a large crowd of local citizens as well as foreign visitors of different faiths. They watched in amazement as the illuminated figure knelt before the cross on the largest dome of the church, blessed the people below, and rested in an attitude of prayer.

The apparitions at Zeitoun continued for the next three years, each one lasting a few minutes to a few hours. The visions were photographed by hundreds of photographers and were even captured on Egyptian television. It is estimated that as many as one million people were privileged to witness these silent but powerful apparitions, and that numerous cures and miracles took place in the little suburb. In contrast to the war and chaos in the Middle East, the apparitions at Zeitoun brought together people of different faiths and different ideas in an atmosphere of peace and prayer.

A River of Blood

Africa is a continent that has long been plagued by drought, famine, poverty, and brutal clashes for power between local tribes. In the heart of Africa lies Rwanda, one of its poorest countries and the site of an important series of apparitions that took place 1981 to 1983. The Virgin Mary, addressing herself as "Mother of the Word," appeared in the impoverished village of Kibeho and spoke to six school-age Catholic girls and a pagan boy about terrible future events that would happen if the world did not repent of its ways and turn back to God. The world was on the edge of catastrophe, the Virgin told the young people, and there was not much time left to prepare for the Last Judgment. She had come to ready the way for her Son and to invite the world to prayer, fasting, and penance.

The visions attracted the attention of the local people, who had grown lazy in their practice of Catholicism. They were amazed at the deep state of rapture of the visionaries and how they showed no reaction to the touch of a burning match or a knife prick to their skin during their trances. The visionaries reported being taken mystically to heaven, hell, and purgatory, and they were visibly moved by these experiences. The most traumatic vision, however, lasted a full eight hours and frightened even the onlookers. The visionaries were told of a great tragedy that would hit Rwanda if the tiny nation did not turn back to God. They were shown terrifying visions of trees in flames, people killing one another, a river of blood, and corpses scattered everywhere—many without heads.

This prophetic warning came true for the country ten years later, when a bloody civil war broke out between the local Hutu and Tutsi tribes. The fighting left one million dead. Butchered bodies, too numerous to bury, were cast into the river, turning the water a deep red. Today, the people of Rwanda have renewed faith, but they still suffer from poverty, disease, and a harsh government. The country did not take seriously the warnings it had been given. Will the rest of the world make the same mistake?

✠   ✠   ✠

As I write this, apparitions continue to be reported from around the world. There have been claims of such visitations in Ireland, Switzerland, the Ukraine, Bosnia-Herzegovina (the former Yugoslavia), Venezuela, and numerous locations in the United States—just to name a few.

Now, before you run off at the next report of someone seeing Mary in his garage, I want to close this chapter with a few warnings of my own. There are lots of people today who would just love to say they've seen something special or that a "heavenly visitor" has given them crucial messages for the world. But the reality is, genuine apparitions happen to people who aren't looking for them. In fact, visionaries sometimes wish later that they had never received the apparitions, because of the huge responsibility that comes with this particular gift. Therefore, if you hear a "visionary" giving interviews on the evening news and happily rattling off specific dates of gloom and doom, simply change the channel.

Also, genuine apparitions happen to whomever God chooses—not necessarily to the person *we* think would make a good visionary. Bernadette Soubirous of Lourdes was the last person in her town anyone would have chosen to receive visits from the Mother of God. Still, she was chosen, and her supernatural visions helped her grow immensely in holiness. But neither does every visionary become deeply holy and humble. Melanie Matthieu, another French child who saw the Virgin Mary just twelve years before Bernadette, in the town of La Salette, France, had quite the opposite experience. She was considered a pious young girl before her apparition, but afterward she became a spoiled brat, running around Europe and demanding that everyone treat her like a saint. That doesn't discount her visions, which the Church has approved, but it shows you just how fragile human nature can be when you're on the other end of the "spiritual telephone" with God.

Also important to keep in mind: it's not our job to give our personal stamp of approval to reports of apparitions, no matter how believable they seem to be. Let the Church, which has both the expertise and authority to discern them, figure it out. And give them time—some apparitions weren't approved until a century or more after they took place! Finally, please use common sense. Although there are lots of references in the Bible about the appearance of heavenly messengers, there isn't a single example of someone's face appearing on a flower petal or on a piece of food. (So if you're thinking of making a bid on eBay for that grilled-cheese sandwich with Mary's likeness on it, don't.)

Remember that everything God ever needed to tell us about Christianity has already been revealed (at least implicitly) in Holy Scripture and taught by Christ's Church. Nothing new needs to be added. The private revelations in this chapter do not give us something new to believe in: these visions simply serve to remind us of our faith and to strengthen it. If you need the reminder, take it. Then, focus your sight on the Bible and the sacraments. Get the picture?

CHAPTER 6

A Far Cry From the Ordinary: Weeping Statues and Images

For many live as enemies of the cross of Christ; I have often told you of them, and now I tell you even with tears.

—Philippians: 3:18

Walk into any Catholic Church anywhere in the world, and you'll probably find at least one statue. The older the church, the more statues you tend to find. Yes, we Catholics certainly love our statues—we even keep them in our homes and gardens. For some of our non-Catholics friends, this can pose a bit of a problem. After all, they may ask, doesn't the Bible warn against "graven images"?

The image itself is not the problem—although the attitude toward it can be. Let me explain. If you had a favorite grandfather you dearly loved who was no longer

alive, would it be acceptable for you to hang a picture of
him in your home? Of course. When you look at the picture, does it remind you of him and the good times you
shared together? Does it sometimes cause an emotion
inside of you that makes you smile or even cry? If you are
human, the answer to both questions is yes.

But if you began to think that the picture was actually
your grandfather, that's when you'd have to stop and grab
hold on the reins of reality. The picture is *not* your grandfather. Neither are the statues in your parish actually Jesus
or Mary or Saint Patrick, or any kind of god or goddess or
spiritual power. The statues in our churches, and the *icons*
(a Greek word for image) that hang in Eastern Rite churches
are there to inspire us and *remind* us of the holy ones that
deserve our reverence and respect, not to replace them.

It's perfectly okay to pray in the presence of a statue
of Jesus, for example, to decorate it with flowers, or to
even kiss it tenderly, as long as we remember that we
are not worshiping the statue itself, but the God it rep-
resents. (And, just to clarify, we reserve worship for God
alone. As for Mary and the other saints, we give them our
deep reverence, but *not* our worship. That's a huge difference, so please make a note of it!)

It's important to be clear about the purpose of statues and artwork in the Catholic faith, both for your own
understanding and for the sake of others who may ask
you about it. More importantly, we must keep these facts
straight in our heads when we add a supernatural dimen-
sion to the subject, such as when statues and artwork begin
doing things that ordinary statues and artwork shouldn't
be doing: for example, weeping blood, sweat, or tears.

It may surprise you to read that reports of weeping
statues, and to a lesser degree, weeping paintings, are
actually fairly common in the Catholic Church. Approval

of these events, however, is far less common. That's because there is often a natural explanation for the occurrence, such as condensation forming on the cracks of a statue. Other times it can be the result of an elaborate hoax on the part of a sadly confused individual. Therefore, the Catholic Church is very hesitant about making any official statements in these matters. (The Orthodox Church, on the other hand, takes a different approach. If an object is reported to be shedding tears, an *exorcism* (a formal ritual for expelling demons) is performed on it. If the object continues weeping, the faithful are permitted (but not required) to venerate it.)

But here's where we need to keep things in perspective. Even with the blessing of Mother Church, the objects involved in the following stories are still only objects. They may be considered worthy of our veneration, *but not for themselves alone.* Rather, we should consider them instruments of God's grace and outward signs for believers and non-believers alike. It's what's *behind* these intriguing events (at least in the authentic cases) that requires our attention, our reflection, and our response. With that in mind, we are now ready to delve into the final category in our study of the mystical aspects of the Catholic faith.

The Weeping Woodcut

Weeping statues and images can be found throughout the world, but the most common location seems to be Italy. Perhaps the earliest weeping image on record dates back to 1498, in the small Italian village of Bagno di Romagna. At the time there was a great deal of fighting in the town, which inspired a devout family in the village to gather before a small woodcut image of the Blessed Mother holding the Baby Jesus in her arms, and pray earnestly for peace.

One night, as the father of the household was lighting his lamp to begin prayers, he noticed a trickle of blood flowing down the arm of the Virgin. He called his family at once. Soon the townspeople discovered the news and began to arrive at the home to witness the miracle for themselves. Falling on their knees before the tiny picture, they begged one another for forgiveness. The miracle lasted about two hours, long enough for the entire town to come and be reconciled. The entire town, that is, with the exception of two men who had been involved in a long-term feud. Although the blood on the image had stopped flowing, the villagers insisted that the two remaining men come to see the image and hear about the miraculous event. When they entered the room, two drops of blood appeared on the arm of the Madonna. The men were convinced at once and made peace with each other. The image was encased in an elaborate silver frame and moved to the Basilica of Santa Maria Assunta, the town church, where it still is displayed today.

Sobbing in Syracuse

Three centuries later, a similar miracle occurred in the city of Syracuse, on the island of Sicily, part of what today is Italy. The Greeks were the first civilization to inhabit Syracuse, and they built a marvelous city there. Its beautiful architecture and prime location on the Mediterranean Sea caught the attention of many invaders, including the Romans, Moors, Turks, Normans, and Spanish. The city also fell victim to disastrous earthquakes and a deadly plague. In 1719, as the Spanish took their turn at attacking the city, the inhabitants of Syracuse pleaded with St. Lucy, their patron saint. A marble statue of the saint in the city is said to have shed abundant tears for days. Unfortunately, the miracle did not stop the attack of the Spanish, but it made a lasting impression on the faithful.

The Gift That Kept on Giving

Syracuse would be the location of a second and quite popular weeping miracle, in more contemporary times. In 1953, Antonina and Angelo Iannuso received as a wedding gift a plaster plaque of the Immaculate Heart of Mary mounted on a black background. Although the couple were rather neglectful about their faith, they hung the image in their bedroom. Shortly after their marriage, Antonina became pregnant. What should have been a time of bliss became a time of hardship and suffering when Antonina developed a condition called toxemia that caused her to have convulsions and periods of blindness.

On August 29, 1953, in the midst of this difficulty with her health, the young Italian bride noticed to her great astonishment that the Madonna hanging above her bed was weeping tears. Thinking she must be seeing things because of her illness, Antonina summoned her sister-in-law and her aunt, who confirmed that it was not the roof that was leaking, but tears that were falling from the eyes of the Virgin onto the headboard of the bed.

Word spread quickly throughout the city. Crowds gathered in such number to see the image that the family hung it outside their home for the people to venerate. The tears were gathered by the faithful on pieces of cloth and wads of cotton and many of the sick were healed. This included Antonina herself, who regained her health to deliver a bouncing baby boy a few months later.

The bishop was notified about the weeping image and he responded by sending a team of clergymen to investigate the case. They carefully studied the plaster sculpture, removing it from its backing, but they could find no cause for the salty water gathering in the eyes of the Madonna. When the doctors and chemists analyzed the tears in a nearby laboratory, they were found to closely resemble human tears. On the first day of September, four days after the weeping started, the tears stopped, never to be repeated.

After studying the testimonies of the witnesses, the sudden and unexplained healings, and the conclusions of the laboratory, the archbishop of Palermo accepted the event at Syracuse as a miracle. This conclusion was echoed by Pope Pius XII, who asked the question, "Will men understand the mysterious language of these tears?"

Tears, Made in Japan

Another Church-approved miracle took place in 1973 in the small mountain village of Akita, Japan. Agnes Katsuko Sasagawa (try saying *that* one three times fast!), a Catholic convert, was an associate member of a small religious community called the Handmaids of the Eucharist. She prayed with the sisters, but worked and lived outside of the convent. In March 1973, the young woman became totally deaf and was invited to become a live-in member of the community.

Soon after, interesting things began to happen to Sister Agnes. In June, she developed the stigmata on her right hand. One week later, she received the first of three messages while praying in the presence of a three-foot tall wooden statue of Our Lady. The statue seemed to come alive and was bathed in light, speaking words that Agnes, though deaf, could hear and understand. The Virgin predicted that Agnes's deafness would be healed and asked the nun to offer all of her sufferings for the sins of the world.

A week after this apparition, the statue, like Sister Agnes, began to bleed from the right palm. Soon after, blood appeared on the statue's face, neck, hands, and feet. Meanwhile, Sister Agnes' pain became almost unbearable. On August 3, she received a second message from the statue. She was told that a great chastisement would be inflicted by the Heavenly Father, and that prayer, penance, and sacrifices could soften his anger at the neglect of humankind.

In late September, the statue began to perspire a liquid that smelled wonderfully of flowers. Then, on October 13 (the anniversary of the great miracle at Fatima), Sister Agnes received a third and final message. The Virgin, echoing the words of Scripture, foretold of a time when fire would fall from the sky, wiping out a great part of humanity. She talked about how the evil one will infiltrate even the Church, pitting cardinal against

The weeping statue of Akita.
Photo courtesy of the 101 Foundation.

cardinal and bishop against bishop. The rosary, as she said in many previous apparitions, was a powerful tool against the evil one. On October 13 the following year, Sister Agnes miraculously regained her hearing, just as the Virgin had predicted.

It's said that the statue at Akita wept tears a total of 101 times over the course of seven years. More than 500 people witnessed these tears, including the local bishop, and numerous medical cures were reported. When the statue's mysterious fluids were analyzed scientifically, they were found to be human tears, sweat, and blood. After an intense investigation lasting three years, Bishop Ito of Nigata, Japan, declared the events at Akita to be miraculous. Cardinal Joseph Ratzinger (who would become Pope Benedict XVI) affirmed in 1988 that the phenomenon was reliable and worthy of belief.

A Child Shall Lead Them

Reports of weeping statues and images can also be found in the United States. One of the most prominent cases is that of Audrey Marie Santo of Worcester, Massachusetts. In 1987, three-year-old Audrey fell into her family swimming pool and nearly drowned. When she was rushed to the hospital, doctors over-medicated the child, which caused her to lapse into a coma for three weeks. Although she regained consciousness, she was no longer able to speak or move for the rest of her life.

News spread quickly about the tragedy, as Audrey's situation was publicized in newspaper articles and on television. Hundreds of people of different faiths were inspired to visit the bedridden girl during the four months she remained in the hospital. Countless others joined in praying for a miracle. Although the medical professionals recommended that Audrey be placed in an institution, her family would not hear of it. Instead, they brought the little girl home where they cared for her with deep faith and love.

Visitors continued to pray at the bedside of the child at her small home. Two years after Audrey's accident, mysterious things began to happen. At first, a powerful scent of roses could be smelled in her bedroom. Then, nurses caring for Audrey noticed that during the season of Lent, her heart rate and breathing would increase during the afternoon hours (the time Jesus hung on the Cross), and that she seemed to be in great discomfort. Mysterious wounds resembling those of Christ began to appear on her hands, feet, side, and head. At other times, Audrey seemed to take on symptoms of the physical illnesses of her visitors, and numerous people claimed to be cured after their visit. The more these unusual incidents were reported, the more people came to see the child.

In 1994, an image of Our Lady of Guadalupe displayed on the piano of the Santo home began to drip sweet-smelling oil. In time, more than three dozen statues, paintings, and other holy objects in and around Audrey's bedroom also began to weep tears of oil and blood. The bishop commissioned a laboratory to test the oil: some of it was found to be a pure form of olive oil, while much of the rest of it was of an unknown origin. Over the years, the mysterious fluid has been collected and distributed to the faithful and has been said to bring about further healings.

Audrey was kept alive through a special tube inserted into her stomach, since she could not swallow solid food through her mouth. However, on her First Holy Communion, she was able to receive the Holy Eucharist on her tongue, and she received it that way daily for the rest of her life. The Bishop of Worcester gave his permission for a tabernacle to be installed in Audrey's bedroom, and on five separate occasions, hosts that were consecrated at the Santo home were seen to bleed.

A team of psychologists, doctors, and a theologian was commissioned to formally investigate the events surrounding Audrey Santo. The first phase of the investigation ruled out any form of trickery regarding the weeping statues and images. However, the cause and purpose of these mysterious fluids is yet to be determined. In addition, more investigation needs to be done on the miraculous claims of healing said to have occurred in Audrey's presence.

On April 14, 2007, at the age of 23, Audrey Santo passed away peacefully from cardiac arrest after twenty years of witnessing silently to faith and suffering. The statues and images in her bedroom continue to weep, and her case continues to be investigated. By the world's standards, a person such as Audrey would be considered a burden and an unproductive member of society. But to those who knew and loved her, she was a gift and a chosen instrument of God. Without words or actions, Audrey taught the world an important lesson—that human life is valuable in any form.

Tears of Blood

We began our study of weeping statues and icons in Italy, and that's where we'll conclude, with the story of an event that started in 1995 in the small port city of Civitavecchia, some forty miles north of Rome. Many families in the region had left their Catholic faith to become Jehovah's Witnesses. The parish priest, a Spaniard named Father Pablo Santiago, did much with his prayers and powerful witness to win people back to the Catholic Church. One of the families he helped was that of an electrician named Fabio Gregori. When the family's son took ill, Father Pablo brought him a statue of the Madonna he had purchased on a pilgrimage to Bosnia-Herzegovina (the former Yugoslavia) where reported apparitions were taking place. Fabio received the statue from the priest with gratitude and built a little shrine for it in the family's yard.

One day, the family's six-year-old daughter, Jessica, who liked to decorate the shrine with flowers each day, noticed that the statue was crying brownish-red tears. Soon the Gregorio home was swamped with curious visitors. When Bishop Girolano Grillo heard the news, he was quite skeptical. There were reports that some people in the town were practicing devil worship, and he was not willing to take any chances. Therefore, he instructed the parish priest to destroy the statue with a hammer. But the priest could not bring himself to do it, and delivered the statue to Bishop Grillo instead. When the bishop held the statue in his hands, it began to weep tears. Instantly, he believed. (That must have made the statue happy, for it was the last time it would cry.)

A formal investigation was begun, and the tears of blood were confirmed to be human male blood. (That seems to illustrate our point earlier about how Mary always points to her son, Jesus.) According to the bishop, numerous miraculous events have taken place since the statue at Civitavecchia began shedding tears. These include cures of cancer and drug addiction, saved marriages, and conversions of Jehovah's Witnesses as well as radical political members. At present, a Vatican commission is further investigating the case of Civitavecchia. Meanwhile, hundreds of thousands of pilgrims have visited the little statue through the years, which today is housed in the parish church.

✠   ✠   ✠

Why all the tears? And why are they so often shed by images of the Mother of God? Although the tears themselves are silent, they send a loud message of profound sadness. When the tears consist of blood, the cry seems to be all the more urgent.

If we recall the life of Mary of Nazareth, we remember that she had her fair share of sorrows. She might have faced rejection and ridicule for becoming pregnant outside of marriage. She was forced to bear her child in the wilderness and forced to flee to another country to keep him from being killed by a jealous king. All too soon, her son left home to begin his mission, and Mary's heart, as predicted by the prophet, Simeon, was pierced by a sword as she followed her son to Calvary.

As mother of us all, Mary continues to care for her children around the world and throughout the ages. She cries like our earthly mothers do when we stubbornly wander from the right path. In various apparitions the Virgin has appeared in great sorrow, telling visionaries that time is running out for the world if it does not turn back to God. She tells us that she will not be able to hold back the hand of God's justice forever. Each person who is in jeopardy of losing heaven is a great sorrow to her, and the supernatural signs of tears on statues and artwork cry out for our attention. Will we respond to these tears with prayer and repentance, or will we, as St. Paul says in the opening quote of this chapter, live as enemies of the Cross of Christ?

CHAPTER 7

Where Do We Go from Here?

Blessed are those who have not seen, and yet have come to believe.

—John 20:29

Bleeding hands. Bleeding Hosts. Dead bodies that refuse to rot. Saints who can fly. Visions that warn, and statues that weep. We've certainly covered some amazing subjects in our brief time together. This book, however, is meant only to be an introduction to such events. If these stories intrigue you, there are plenty of books out there that cover them—and others—in greater depth. At the end of this book is a suggested reading list that will give you a good starting point from which to learn more about the topics that interest you most. You can take it from there.

Before I let you go, however, I'd like to leave you with a few concluding thoughts about the mysterious subject of the supernatural.

Natural *is Super, Too!*

The events described in this book—as spectacular as they may be—are not any better or any more important than the daily, ordinary experiences of God available to each one of us. Every day presents a new opportunity to experience God in the people, places, and situations around us. We don't *have* to travel across the globe to seek miracles. All we have to do is open our eyes and look around. Genuine mystical experiences of God are available in everyday life!

Some Mysteries are Not Meant to be Solved

We are far too limited as human beings ever to understand the ways of our Creator. God does things in his own way as he sees fit, with his infinite wisdom and justice and mercy. It's not for us to get caught up in the how's and why's of mystical happenings, but rather to grow in our faith and appreciate how great our God is and how much he loves us. The next time we're tempted to try and solve God's mysteries, we ought to use that energy to try and solve the problems in our own lives that may be blocking our relationship with him.

If it Doesn't Point to God, it's Pointless

If a supernatural event doesn't lead us into a deeper relationship with the Holy Trinity (Father, Son, and Holy Spirit), it isn't worth our time or attention. In fact, it can even do us harm. All revelations of God, public and private, *must* lead to him. So, for example, if a supernatural phenomenon (past or present) makes us want to go to Mass more to receive Jesus, if it makes us want to pray more and make sacrifices, if it makes us want to read the Bible more and make changes in ourselves that we know we need to—these are good signs that we are on the right path. If, on the other hand, we want to spend more time reading about certain people, places, or events just for the thrill, we need to adjust our spiritual compass.

Even Saints Can Make Mistakes

We also have to keep in mind that human beings are imperfect. We all make mistakes, and that's true even with saints and visionaries. Some predictions made by the holiest of people have proven flat-out wrong. St. Vincent Ferrer (1350–1419), whom we met in chapter four, spent the last twenty-one years of his life preaching that the end of the world was at hand. He even brought back to life a dead woman for a few minutes just to confirm his prediction. Obviously, the end of the world did not happen. As convincing as Vincent was, he was dead wrong on this one.

Also, what may start out to look like a good thing can quickly turn unproductive or even contrary to our faith. Two reports of apparitions in our own country in the past twenty-five years—from Bayside, New York, and Scottsdale, Arizona—have both been rejected by the Catholic Church because of the questionable nature of the seers and the troublesome messages they conveyed. The fact is, being a channel for God in a public way is a tremendous responsibility, and sometimes people in that position find out they just can't do the job. That's why Jesus left us his Church on earth; so that we might not be led astray.

The Miracle of Belief

To witness something supernatural with our own eyes is both a privilege and a grace. But we receive even more grace when we believe in such things without any physical proof at all. For this, we will be well rewarded! Blessed indeed are those who have not seen, and yet believe.

As followers of Christ, we are called to become believers, especially in an age when unbelief runs high. We are called to be witnesses to all the wonders around us, large and small. While the world rushes on, looking unsuccessfully for hope and joy and peace in all the wrong places, we have already found it in Jesus Christ. Now we have the responsibility of sharing it with others. Our strong belief is the fuel for this mission!

A Final Thought

And now, I would like you to picture yourself standing on a sidewalk in front of the most beautiful cathedral you can imagine. It's an immense building, with carved angels smiling down at you, and ornate spires that reach to the heavens. The sound of bells fills the air. You climb the massive steps of this cathedral and open the great wooden doors to the lobby. Here you discover a beautiful room decorated with stained glass windows and statues and flowers—a marvelous place to behold. You've never seen anything like it, and you wish to stay here forever.

After soaking up the greatness of this magnificent vestibule, you turn to go home; but haven't you forgotten something? Of course you have. You've neglected to open the next set of doors to experience the amazing grandeur *inside*. You would have missed the main part of the cathedral and the reason it was built: to worship Jesus in the Eucharist.

Placing too much emphasis on the extraordinary supernatural events is sort of like setting up camp in the lobby of a great cathedral. It's a wonderful place (and much better than the sidewalk!), but in perspective it's really only a doorway and an invitation into an even grander place, which is the heart of the Church. The *true* miracles and treasures of our faith lie here, where we can come to our Creator in the sacraments, in the word, and in the liturgy. Now that you know that little secret, go ahead and pull your friends in off the sidewalk. Share this book with them. Dazzle them with the lobby. Then, make them eager to open the next set of doors so that they, too, can enter more deeply into their Catholic faith and discover the truth, the beauty, and the joy that awaits them. See you inside!

Additional Reading

If you would like to read more about any of the subjects covered in this book, I highly recommend the following books and websites:

Eucharistic Miracles

Eucharistic Miracles by Joan Carroll Cruz
Illinois: Tan Books and Publishers, Inc., 1987.

Secrets of the Eucharist by Michael H Brown
Ohio: Faith Publishing Company, 1966.

This is My Body, This is My Blood: Miracles of the Eucharist by Bob and Penny Lord
California: Journeys of Faith Publishing, 1986.

The Real Presence
www.therealpresence.com

The Stigmata

Stigmata: A Medieval Phenomenon in a Modern Age by Ted Harrison
New York: St. Martin's Press, 1994.

Stigmata: An Investigation into the Mysterious Appearance of Christ's Wounds in Hundreds of People from Medieval Italy to Modern America by Ian Wilson
San Francisco: Harper & Row, 1989.

They Bore the Wounds of Christ: The Mystery of the Sacred Stigmata by Michael Freze
Indiana: Our Sunday Visitor Publishing, 1989.

Myrna Nazzour official website
www.soufanieh.com/menuenglish.htm

Incorrupt Bodies

The Incorruptibles by Joan Carroll Cruz
Illinois: Tan Books and Publishers, 1997.

Incorrupt Bodies of the Saints
http://members.aol.com/ccmail/incorruptbodies.html

Amazing Saints

Mysteries, Marvels, Miracles: In the Lives of the Saints by Joan Carroll
    Cruz
Illinois: Tan Books and Publishers, 1997.

Mystics & Miracles: True Stories of Lives Touched by God by Bert
    Ghezzi
Illinois: The Loyola Press, 2004.

The Mystical Body: An Investigation of Supernatural Phenomena By
    Patricia Treece
New York: The Crossroad Publishing Company, 2005.

Apparitions

A Still, Small Voice: A Practical Guide on Reported Apparitions by
    Father Benedict Groeschel
San Francisco: Ignatius Press, 1993.

*Apparitions, Healings, and Weeping Madonnas: Christianity and the
    Paranormal* by Lisa J. Schwebel
New Jersey: Paulist Press, 2004.

Fatima: The Story Behind the Miracles By Renzo and Roberto Allegri
Ohio: St. Anthony Messenger Press, 2001.

Lourdes: Font of Faith, Hope, & Charity By Elizabeth Ficocelli
New Jersey: Paulist Press, 2007.

Voices, Visions, and Apparitions By Michael Freze
Indiana: Our Sunday Visitor Publishing, 1993.

The Official Fatima Website
www.santuario-fatima.pt

The Official Lourdes Website
www.lourdes-france.org

Weeping Statues

Miraculous Images of Our Lady: 100 Famous Catholic Statues and Portraits by Joan Carroll Cruz
Tan Books and Publishing, 1994.

(video) *Tears From Heaven.* Marian Communications. Lincoln University, PA. 2000.

(video) *Audrey's Life: Voice of a Silent Soul.* The Mercy Foundation. St. Louis, MO, 1996.

Audrey Santo official website
www.littleaudreysanto.org/

Website about Julia Kim
www.marys-touch.com/introduction/miracles.htm

About the Author

Elizabeth Ficocelli is a best-selling, award-winning author of ten books for adults and young people. Her books include *Lourdes: Font of Faith, Hope & Charity; The Fruits of Medjugorje: Stories of True and Lasting Conversion; The Imitation of Christ for Children* (Paulist Press); and *Shower of Heavenly Roses: Stories of the Intercession of St. Therese of Lisieux* (The Crossroad Publishing Company). A Catholic convert and mother of four, Elizabeth is a frequent guest on Catholic radio and television. She is also a popular speaker at conferences, parish retreats, and schools.